# ANNENBERG

# ANNENBERG

## A Biography of Power

BY GAETON FONZI

WEYBRIGHT AND TALLEY
NEW YORK

Published in the United States by
WEYBRIGHT AND TALLEY, INC.
3 EAST 54TH STREET
NEW YORK, NEW YORK 10022.

BOOK DESIGN BY BENTE HAMANN

Library of Congress Catalog Card Number: 76-106028

Printed in the United States of America

PHOTO CREDITS
Page 3, Underwood and Underwood;
page 6, Wide World;
page 7, Central Press (Pictorial Parade).

# CONTENTS

# Foreword

I believe Walter Annenberg's finest contribution to American journalism was revealed on October 28, 1969. That was the day it was announced he was selling the Philadelphia *Inquirer* and *Daily News* to the John S. Knight chain.

I believe he sold them because he no longer needed them. He had used them to achieve the power, prestige and social acceptability that led to his crowning ambition, appointment as the United States Ambassador to England. His record of subordinating journalistic principles to that ambition had become a tainted burden.

I also believe that Walter Annenberg never possessed the personal qualifications or knowledge of foreign affairs to merit appointment as the Ambassador to England. The fact that he was appointed reflects unfavorably on the American political system and on President Richard Nixon.

Those are only my beliefs, but as a journalist and an American citizen I feel strongly about them and they have undoubtedly affected the viewpoint of this study. But I hope that my compassion for the man and my faith in the political system are also reflected in that viewpoint.

Other than that, you should know that this book was derived from a series of articles in *Philadelphia Magazine,* an independent local publication. This is most apparent in the italicized sections, which deal with my atttempts to obtain a personal interview with Annenberg. They could have been eliminated, but they reveal something fascinating about the man and provide an insight into my approach to him.

I am appreciative, of course, to D. Herbert Lipson, the publisher of *Philadelphia Magazine,* and Alan Halpern, its editor, for their encouragement and support in every way.

G. F.

# PART ONE

# THE PARLAY

Walter Hubert Annenberg has made it.

He has emerged from the dark shadow of private turmoil to the bright sanctity of international prestige and respectability.

As imperious editor and publisher of the Philadelphia *Inquirer*—and absolute monarch of an awesome communications empire—he has been one of Philadelphia's most powerful men. And one of the nation's wealthiest.

Now he is a confidant of the President of the United States.

Now he is ambassador to the Court of St. James's.

Yet Walter Hubert Annenberg remains shrouded in mystery. No one has ever attempted to remove that shroud. That is the way Walter Annenberg wanted it.

And what Walter Annenberg wants, Walter Annenberg gets.

∘ ∘ ∘

*Walter Annenberg leaned back in his chair and laughed. He was sitting behind a big oak desk in his twelfth-floor office in the Inquirer Building a few weeks before he was scheduled to depart for England. His office is neither ornate nor somber. It is, in fact, an expansive office, light and airy, with a sky-blue rug and a white couch and tables and shelves neatly cluttered with framed photographs and plaques.*

*"Some of those questions you submitted," he chuckled, motioning to my letter on his desk, "I mean, let's not be juvenile. You know the type I mean. The when-did-you-stop-beating-your-wife type. There were a few of those in there, you know." He laughed heartily. He was obviously delighted at having detected those questions and enjoyed laying it on the line, one journalist to another.*

*I laughed back, myself delighted that he found his own perceptiveness so amusing. I had been told he was basically a humorless man. Yes, I said, I could see how he might consider some of the questions to be of that type, but they were based on assumptions drawn from available information, not from any real knowledge of his motivations. Those have always been something of a mystery. In fact, the question of Walter Annenberg's motivations has recurrently puzzled many Philadelphians down through the years. Not really knowing, people have often assumed the worst.*

*He leaned forward. He is a trim, stocky man, not tall, with broad shoulders and chunky hands. His face is strong, tanned, with dark eyes that get very serious. "You must remember," he said, speaking slowly and deliberately, "there are many human beings in this world with psychiatric problems who tend to see others in terms of those problems. These are sick, pinched-up, unfortunate human beings full of hate and resentment who like to ascribe to others their own unfortunate characteristics. They view my motivations in terms of their own sickness. I feel sorry for such people."*

∘ ∘ ∘

It is not an easy thing to understand Walter Annenberg. A seamless web of myths and canards surrounds the man. He has striven to be one of the important figures in American journalism, yet he has long disdainfully avoided close journalistic scrutiny. The interviews he has granted down through the years have been deliberately few, curt, and superficial. Once asked if he would cooperate for a comprehensive, in-depth profile, he brusquely replied: "I don't want publicity, I *give* publicity."

Only Walter Annenberg could have gotten away with it. There are few men in the United States with as much wealth and power about whom so little is known. One of the reasons Annenberg has been able to avoid notoriety over the years is that he controlled two of the three daily newspapers in the city from which such notoriety might have emanated. He also controls one of three major tele-

vision stations. And its top-rated radio station. Millions
of people in one of the nation's vital metropolitan areas
rely on news outlets controlled by Walter Annenberg.

Just how important such control can be was pointed
out recently by Federal Communications Commissioner
Nicholas Johnson writing in the *Atlantic:* "What we
sometimes fail to realize . . . is the political significance
of the fact that we have become a nation of cities. Nearly
half of the American people live in the six largest states:
California, New York, Illinois, Pennsylvania, Texas, and
Ohio. Those states, in turn, are substantially influenced
(if not politically dominated) by their major population-
industrial-financial-media centers, such as Los Angeles,
New York City, Chicago, and Philadelphia—the nation's
four largest metropolitan areas. Thus, to have a major
newspaper or television station influence in *one* of these
cities is to have significant national power."

Walter Annenberg has used his Philadelphia-based
communications empire to achieve a measure of that
"significant national power," as well as the prestige and
social recognition that comes with it. Not that he has
ever used the media he controls for blatant personal publicity. He has always been carefully subtle that way. The
Philadelphia *Inquirer,* for instance, handled the announcement of his appointment as ambassador to Great
Britain with ridiculous diffidence, relegating a small portrait of its publisher to the third page along with those of
the two other ambassadors appointed the same day. The
*Daily News,* his other paper, couldn't bury the announcement any deeper, at the bottom of its second page under

the headline "EARLY SENATE APPROVAL SEEN FOR THREE KEY ENVOY POSTS." His radio stations, WFIL-AM and FM, carried it as just another brief item on their news reports. Only a relatively new arrival in Philadelphia, a redheaded newscaster named Al McDowell of WFIL-TV, handled the story as if a Philadelphia news outlet might legitimately have more than casual interest in the appointment of a Philadelphian to an international post —even if the appointee owned the outlet. McDowell, in fact, got an unprecedented but brief interview with his boss, who carefully read a statement from a cue card. Although McDowell was later dropped by the station and quietly left town (most likely for reasons irrelevant here), his interview suggested the probably painful but deliberate acknowledgment by Annenberg that the price of his new, prestigious position would include more public scrutiny than he had ever before subjected himself to.

The fact that he has eschewed the spotlight has not kept Walter Annenberg from being one of the predominant men in the power structures that rule Philadelphia. Politicians of both parties have, down through the years, gone to him with hat in hand to ask his support and a few, failing to get it, have reconsidered their ambitions. No important public programs are launched without considering what his views on them will be. Civic movements and citizens' committees weigh his opinion heavily in charting their courses of action. Cultural and charitable organizations vie for his favor. Individuals with aspirations of success in any public field ignore his presence and power at their peril. Walter Annenberg has made men, and he has broken men.

For more than thirty years Annenberg has attempted to inject himself into the community with a dedicatory fervor. He has striven to assume a role as one of Philadelphia's principal benefactors. He has used his newspapers to battle the demons of injustice and evil, crime and corruption, whenever and wherever he thought they threatened. He has donated millions of dollars to organized charities and sponsored numerous sporting, musical, dramatic, and cultural events for their causes. He has been a strong supporter of the Philadelphia Museum and the Philadelphia Orchestra. He has given to hospitals, medical-research facilities, and a variety of religious institutions. He has been extremely generous to a number of local colleges and universities and taken an active interest in the area's educational assets. He has, in sum, attempted to establish himself as a positive force in his community.

Yet Walter Annenberg's image, gossamery as it is, isn't primarily one of the beneficent philanthropist.

There are, in fact, men in his hometown who despise him with a burning intensity.

There are more than a few who are outraged at what they feel has been his repeated misuse of his power.

Many consider him a withdrawn, erratic, overreacting demagogue.

And there are those, including a number on the very newspapers he owned, who are convinced he has been one of the most detestable and detrimental men in journalism today.

Most of all, Walter Annenberg is a man to be treated with a great deal of deference, and perhaps even to be feared. Many are simply awed at the force he can wield and consider him prone to wield it at the slightest provocation.

"He is not a guy I would want to get mad at me," said a top political figure.

One of Annenberg's close associates, a prominent Philadelphian long known for his fierce spirit of independence and for voicing his opinions with fearless and sometimes reckless candor, refused to even talk about Annenberg, on or off the record. "My *God*," he said, "I'd be out of my mind!"

And even a national publication, reporting his ambassadorial appointment, noted: "Annenberg is known in Philadelphia as a tough man to cross." That was softened from the phrase the publication's reporter had used in a background memo to his editor. Annenberg, he had written, has a reputation for being "a vindictive son-of-a-bitch."

∘ ∘ ∘

When Annenberg has revealed himself it has been largely through his role as editor and publisher of the Philadelphia *Inquirer*. There are other owners of newspapers who take the title of editor, but there are few who have taken it as seriously. It is the way he handled that job that has adulterated to a great extent his vigorous attempts to become a respected, positive force in the community.

Walter Annenberg always considered the *Inquirer* the most prized, although not the most profitable, legacy of his father, Moses L. Annenberg. It certainly was *the* steppingstone in his climb to international status. He might not have even begun to hobnob with national politicians and world statesmen if he hadn't been the owner of a major urban newspaper. "Without the *Inquirer*," Annenberg once confided to a friend, "I'd be just another millionaire."

It is one of the tragedies of Walter Annenberg's life that despite his achievements, despite his financial successes and his great philanthropies, he is known as a man who has used the power of the press as a personal weapon to crack anyone who rubs him the wrong way, disagrees with his opinion or philosophy, or threatens his interests.

Annenberg became editor and publisher of the *Inquirer* at the death of his father in 1942. He was thirty-four years old. He immediately ran this signed announcement on the newspaper's front page:

> To the legion of friends who have expressed their sympathy to my family and to me in our bereavement, I extend my grateful acknowledgements.
>
> The loss is great but I shall carry on, as my father wished me to do, striving always to uphold the great traditions of The Philadelphia Inquirer, founded in 1829, and reaching its point of greatest influence under my father's direction.
>
> Philadelphia is my home. Here I intend to live for the

rest of my life, devoting my best energies to advancing the welfare of our City, our State and my fellow-citizens.

There will be no changes in personnel and with complete unity of purpose we will continue to work together in maintaining the standards and ideals of an independent newspaper for all the people.

There is no doubt that Walter Annenberg was determined to make the *Inquirer* one of the best newspapers in the country, and perhaps in the world. He wanted it to be the standard of excellence and respectability, a journalistic paragon admired both within and outside the profession, unswerving in its objectivity, loyal to its public trust, innovative, exciting but responsible in its news gathering and presentation, a lodestar for the nation's very best talent.

He did not succeed.

The Philadelphia *Inquirer,* by any standard, is not one of the finest newspapers in the country.

There are those who think it is one of the worst. Probably few, if any, newspapermen would rate it above mediocre. That is one of the reasons it had been increasingly difficult for it to attract experienced and talented professionals. As one of its own editors recently said: "Like a dirty ship in the Navy, word gets around."

Whether he realizes it or not—and there is a question about that—Walter Annenberg made the *Inquirer* what it was. He is largely responsible for the standards it approached and the reputation it has attained.

He is also responsible for helping to create the conditions which brought the newspaper a shame and disgrace few other publications have suffered in the history of journalism. For many years the *Inquirer* had harbored one of the nation's most successful blackmailing reporters. It is difficult to cite another newspaper on which he would have survived for so long.

∘ ∘ ∘

*I had first written to Walter Annenberg more than a year ago. I told him I wanted to do an extensive feature article on Triangle Publications, Inc. It would include his own part in the growth and expansion of the corporation and an examination of his basic attitudes and philosophy. I asked to discuss the project with him.*

*"You are probably aware of the statements circulating in various quarters," he wrote back, "indicating that it is the intention of your magazine to do a negative approach feature story on Triangle. This, of course, would be consistent with the attitude your magazine has taken whenever any aspect of Triangle's operations is reviewed."*

*He said he therefore wanted a list of questions submitted in writing. "I shall reply if they are in order," he added. "This may serve to limit the area of misinterpretation and misunderstanding."*

*He signed his reply, as he does all his letters, on a line typed specifically to hold his signature. It is a very tight signature, very low and compact, not at all open or smoothly flowing.*

∘ ∘ ∘

What he made of the Phliadelphia *Inquirer* is part
of the story of Walter Annenberg's character, a part that
will be examined in more detail later. Still, it is only a
part. And perhaps the more significant aspects are reflected in the fact that he is, indeed, creating an admirable
philanthropic legacy; that he has achieved awesome financial success; that he has built an impressive and highly
regarded reputation in the fields of communications and
national publications; and that he had to overcome tremendous personal handicaps, private tragedies, and oner-
ous public and social obstacles to achieve the stature and
recognition that might have come a lot easier to someone
who wasn't so rich, Jewish, and unwilling to disassociate
himself from a father who had gone to jail.

"I started with an awful lot handed to me," Annenberg
once said. It is to his great credit that he has made what
was handed to him seem, in comparison, piddling to what
he has made of it. Today Triangle Publications, Inc., is
one of the giants of its field. It may not come close to a
giant like the Hearst Corp. (annual sales over $500
million) , yet neither is it that far behind. But what is
most amazing is that there is no other organization of its
size so tightly controlled both in breadth and in depth by
a single individual. Walter Annenberg is the apex of
Triangle.

Because Triangle is a very closed corporation, it is
difficult to get a pinpoint accurate picture of its finances.
Its annual income in 1969 was running close to $235 mil-
lion, ranking it among the top twenty-five of the country's
privately held companies in gross sales. (By comparison,

the New York Times Company, with a few million dollars less in annual income, doesn't do as well.) According to independent credit bureau reports, Triangle's total assets were over $136 million and its tangible net worth close to an impressive $84 million before the sale of the *Inquirer* and *Daily News* for $55 million. (An indication of its growth is that in 1953 Annenberg himself estimated Triangle's worth at $25 million.)

Walter Annenberg is the absolute ruler of Triangle. Although, according to its organizational charts, the corporation is guided by a board of directors and a three-man executive committee from that board, Annenberg is the man who makes the decisions. Of the 4 million shares of issued stock, he is the beneficial holder of 3.5 million shares, close to 87 percent of the voting bloc. (He actually owns at least 51 percent, his seven sisters the rest.) The remainder of the issued stock is held by the Annenberg Fund, his chief charitable foundation, and the Annenberg School of Communications, which he founded for the University of Pennsylvania.

It is impossible to determine exactly how much income Annenberg himself derives from Triangle, but there are facts that hint at an approximation. In 1967, for instance, the Annenberg Fund, which holds only 249,880 shares of Triangle stock—probably less than *one-eighth* of the amount owned by Annenberg personally—reported a dividend income of $1,249,400.

Another indication of Annenberg's personal wealth can be gleaned from the fact that, according to him, he tries to equate the extent of his philanthropy to what he calls his "annual good fortune." Over the years he has given away a tremendous amount of money, probably as much as or more than any other individual in the United States. At the University of Pennsylvania, to which he has given or pledged more than $10 million, he was recently revealed to be the anonymous "Mr. Pennsylvania," the mysterious benefactor who will match dollar-for-dollar alumni donations in excess of previous contributions. He is also the "Mr. X" in a similar plan at the Peddie School, his alma mater prep, where his gifts and pledges have topped $3 million and he has built a couple of major buildings.

It is not necessary, of course, to delve into Annenberg's charitable contributions to point out the extent of his wealth. There are other, less publicized indicators. When he recently sodded a nine-hole golf course around his palatial new estate in the desert near Palm Springs, California, he bought control of the local water company to ensure that it stayed green.

Triangle Publications is, of course, Annenberg's money tree. There is every indication that all of its principal branches are running in the black. It is a much bigger tree now than when his father planted it many years ago. At the death of the elder Annenberg it consisted primarily of the *Inquirer,* the New York *Morning Telegraph* racing paper, five regional editions of the *Daily Racing Form, Screen Guide, Radio Guide,* and a couple of blood-and-guts adventure magazines. (Walter gave one of the latter, *Official Detective,* to the M. L. Annenberg Foundation, which sold it in 1964 to Macfadden-Bartell for

$250,000. *Radio Guide* was discontinued in 1943 because of the paper shortage, and *Screen Guide* was sold in 1947 to Hillman Periodicals.)

Triangle Publications, in addition to its two Philadelphia dailies and its national racing publicatons, also published the weekly *TV Guide* and monthly *Seventeen* magazine.

Besides its Philadelphia radio and television outlets, it also operates WNBF-AM-FM and WNBF-TV in Binghamton, New York; WFBG-AM-FM and WFBG-TV in Altoona, Pennsylvania; WNHC-AM-FM and WNHC-TV in New Haven, Connecticut; KFRE-AM-FM and KFRE-TV in Fresno, California; and WLYH-TV in Lebanon, Pennsylvania. (All the television stations are CBS affiliates except WFIL-TV and WNHC-TV, which carry the ABC network.)

A special Gravure Division of Triangle prints the *Inquirer*'s Sunday supplement, *Today,* as well as *Seventeen* and parts of *TV Guide.*

A wholesale distribution division, Triangle Circulation Co., distributes its magazines as well as those of other publishers and the paperback books of Popular Library. Triangle Home Merchandise does merchandising and promotional tie-ins.

McMurray Publishing Co. Ltd. of Toronto publishes the Canadian editions of the *Daily Racing Form,* while McMurray Printers of Miami does job printing business.

Triangle's cable television holdings include the Empire State Cable TV Co. in Binghamton, New York; New Haven Cable TV in Connecticut; Suburban Cable TV,

Commonwealth Cable TV, and Lebanon Valley Cable TV in Pennsylvania; and Central Cable TV and Fresno Cable TV in California. In addition, it has perhaps a dozen more cable television franchises, and applications for another dozen.

(There were recent indications that Triangle is on the verge of disposing of all its CATV holdings. The decision to do so was perhaps a result of the relatively slow return on investment that cable television operations have shown in some areas; or perhaps a result of the Federal Communications Commission's beginning to frown upon multimedia ownership. It is known that Triangle began actively looking for a buyer for its CATV holdings at about the time word got out that there would be objections filed against the automatic renewal of the license for its most profitable broadcasting outlet, WFIL-TV in Philadelphia.)

The corporation is also, of course, a major real estate holder. It owns most of the property surrounding the Inquirer Building between Thirteenth and Fifteenth Streets, Callowhill to Spring Garden, including the old First Regiment Armory Building on Broad Street. It owns most of the buildings occupied by its publications and broadcasting stations, including *TV Guide*'s modern headquarters building on an eight-acre tract in Radnor, Pennsylvania, the *Morning Telegraph*'s building on Fifty-second Street in New York, and the multimillion-dollar circular oddity that houses WFIL's elaborately equipped broadcasting facilities on gilt-edged City Line Avenue property. Its holdings have also included huge chunks of property in center city Philadelphia, including portions of Penn Center, and West Philadelphia. Triangle once owned the land on which the Bulletin Building now stands.

A few years ago Triangle and the Los Angeles Times-Mirror Company formed a separate corporation in the printing and graphics field, but when the Justice Department began looking into its monopoly aspects Triangle sold out to its partner.

Actually, no one except Annenberg and a very few of his top associates knows all of Triangle's myriad interests, but they have included everything from owning a broadcast equipment manufacturing firm (I.T.A. Electronics) to a share in something called Educasting Systems, a method of teaching by radio. It also owns and operates for its top executives a couple of airplanes, worth at least $2 million, and has its own aviation department to service them. (Annenberg's luxurious flagship, a Lockheed Jetstar, can often be seen at International Airport, identifiable by the plain gold triangle on its tail.)

In addition to Triangle, Walter Annenberg has an interesting collection of other business holdings. He owns, as noted, most of the Tamarisk Water Company of Cathedral City, which keeps his California desert estate from going dry. He is also the largest stockholder of the Penn Central Transportation Company, his shares having been valued at over $13 million. He owns more shares in one of Philadelphia's most influential banks, Girard Trust, than any of its other directors, and enough shares in the Campbell Soup Company to earn him a seat on that board also. (He told the Senate Foreign Relations Committee he was planning to resign these directorships upon assuming his ambassadorial duties, and he did.) Down through the years, however, Annenberg's interests have been fairly eclectic, ranging from a fling in oil wells to a flyer in a Broadway musical revue called *Inside U.S.A.*

All of Annenberg's other interests are, of course, dwarfed by his Triangle holdings. Few other corporations are such rocks of financial strength. A recent credit report noted: "Regular balance sheets obtained from outside sources show a strong financial condition with steadily rising tangible net worth through retained earnings."

o o o

*"I am very well aware of the statements circulating in various quarters indicating that it is the intention of* Philadelphia Magazine *to do a negative approach feature story on Triangle," I wrote back to Walter Annenberg.*

*"It is not an irrational assumption, considering the instances this publication has been critical of various policies and personnel of Triangle over the years.*

*"It is, however, an unfair assumption."*

*I pointed out that the magazine had printed articles over the years that were quite favorable to certain Triangle operations and that it would be difficult to ignore the impressive magnitude of the corporation and the role it has played in the field of communications.*

*I asked Annenberg again for at least the permission to*

*discuss the proposed feature article with him. "I don't*
*want to 'limit the area of misinterpretation or misunder-*
*standing,' " I said, "I want to eliminate it."*
*Annenberg never answered the letter.*

○ ○ ○

Triangle's basic strength derives from the fact that
each of its principal operations is a muscular performer.
Even the *Inquirer* and *Daily News,* which probably return a low profit percentage, were far from unsturdy publications. Yet they may, in comparison, seem like weak
sisters next to the bulging financial huskiness of the
others in the brood.

The racing publications, for instance, are solidly entrenched in their field. The *Daily Racing Form* is a hot
seller at every operating race track in the country, as
well as in Mexico and in Canada, but is really only an
abbreviated version of the *Morning Telegraph.* The
*Morning Telegraph* may be the most respected publication of its kind in the world. It is *the* essential newspaper
for horse racing fans. Multimillions of dollars are wagered
daily based on the information it provides. Each day its
pages are crammed with agate charts detailing the complete history and record of every horse running in a race
that day, a fantastic job of compilation considered so
accurate that the charts are recognized as official by the
Thoroughbred Racing Association and the National
Association of State Racing Commissioners. In addition,
it covers news of the racing world in detail and in depth.
What's going on elsewhere is relegated to a single col-

umn, except for a highly regarded stable of columnists who review movies and plays. (The *Telegraph* had for years, before Moses Annenberg bought it, sought its readers among the horsy and sporty Broadway crowd.)

The *Morning Telegraph* is one of the phenomena of the publishing industry. It is a daily newspaper that sells for seventy-five cents a copy, and sells well. Although it carries little advertising, it is a highly profitable operation. Its circulation fluctuates according to the day of the week and how many tracks are operating, but its weekly circulation is close to 400,000. That would bring a revenue of over $15 million in sales alone. The importance of the racing publications in Triangle's holdings was accented by Annenberg recently, just prior to taking his ambassadorial post in England. He appointed Stewart Hooker, who for years had handled all the racing interests, to the board of directors of Triangle, and was reportedly planning to make him his chief liaison for all his publications while he is in England.

Walter Annenberg likes winners. He has had an excellent record in picking them, *Seventeen* magazine being one of his big ones and another example of the type of publication upon which Triangle's strength rests. Annenberg founded it in 1944. He had noticed that fashion magazines were turning away advertising because of the wartime paper shortage, and decided it would pay to invest in the field before the postwar boom got under way. He sounded out Helen Valentine, promotion director of *Mademoiselle,* about being editor of a new book and she suggested narrowing the field to the teenage fashion market. Annenberg went along with the idea and hit a gold mine.

*Seventeen's* first issue sold 400,000 copies. Today its monthly circulation is over 1.5 million and its promotion department claims an average issue is read by 6.3 million, or over half the teenage girls in the country. For the past sixteen years *Seventeen* has carried more advertising than any other monthly women's magazine. It carried a total of 1,763 ad pages in 1968. (A full-color page, which most of its ads are, costs $10,000.) Its fattest issue weighed more than three pounds.

Running the show at *Seventeen* is Enid Haupt, Walter Annenberg's sister. She took over in 1954 and, judging from the quality of the magazine's content, is doing an excellent job. A tall, handsome, aggressive woman, she doesn't take the post as a familial sinecure. There is no pap in the magazine's editorial approach, no conservative streak in its tone. It digs the teenage scene, calls the shots straight. A recent article detailed the pain of turning off drugs, while a columnist in another issue opined: "Virginity is an outmoded ideal." A rather swinging publication for the Annenberg fold.

But the biggest gem in Triangle's bag is, of course, *TV Guide*. There is no magazine that comes close to it as a rocketing success, not even *Playboy*. And that is saying something. If there ever is a monument to Annenberg's business foresight and his acumen as a publisher, it will be *TV Guide*. To undertake the publishing of a national magazine with local television listings that potential readers were getting for nothing in their newspapers had to take some guts. Annenberg did it in 1953, just when Sunday editions were beginning to come out with their own weekly television listings. Prior to that a scattering of locally owned guides in a few of the major cities were turning a profit by compiling such listings. Annenberg started by buying the biggest of these magazines.

He paid a stiff price for those guides that had already been established in New York, Philadelphia, Washington, Baltimore, and Chicago. Brothers Irvin and Arthur Borowsky of North American Publishing had the Philadelphia book, then called *TV Digest*. Irvin Borowsky says they were grossing about $1.25 million a year with it. A close associate of the brothers claims that they originally refused to sell their publication to Annenberg but Irv Borowsky denies it. He does admit, however, that it would probably have been financially imprudent for them to hold on after Annenberg had captured the New York and Washington publications. He says that Annenberg simply asked him what he wanted for the magazine, he told him, and Annenberg said fine. "There was no haggling at all," he says. "He's not the type to haggle. I'm just sorry I didn't ask for more." The Borowskys still refuse to reveal how much Annenberg paid them for their publication, but if they were grossing as much as they said they were, it could have been close to $400,000.

Annenberg installed the late James Quirk, then the *Inquirer*'s promotion director, as his new entry's publisher, and made the *Inquirer*'s TV critic Merrill Panitt its editor. The first issue of *TV Guide* had ten regional editions. By the end of the first year it had drawn 209 pages of advertising and $750,358 in revenue. It claimed a circulation of 1.5 million.

Today, *TV Guide* is the giant of the weeklies, with its circulation coming close to 15 million, almost twice again as much as *Life*'s. Its advertising revenue has hit an astonishing $60 million. Considering the fact that a fat part of its circulation is through supermarkets, not cut-rate subscriptions, *TV Guide*'s gross income is probably close to $100 million a year.

It's a fantastic operation. Advertisers today are offered a choice of 81 regional editions, printed in fourteen separate printing sites. An editorial staff of 250 compiles local listings in thirty-two offices across the country, are fed network listings by high-speed leased wire from its Radnor headquarters. It appears to be one of Triangle's most efficient operations. An issue that goes on sale in New York on Tuesday is locked up at 12:30 Monday afternoon.

Any diversified corporation would consider a money-maker like *TV Guide* an enviable financial base for all its operations. Yet Triangle has another entry that rivals the magazine as a reliable source of big revenue. In fact, the return from its Radio and Television Division was what gave it the fiscal muscle to get the weekly off the ground.

Annenberg got into the broadcasting business with the purchase of WFIL-AM and FM in 1945. It had resulted from the merger of Philadelphia's first two radio stations, Strawbridge & Clothier's WFI and Lit Brothers' WLIT.

Annenberg paid $190,000 for the outlet, added television to it in 1947.

Today Annenberg's Philadelphia outlets operate out of one of the most modern and technically advanced facilities in the world. Donating its old building and the remains of its equipment (worth about $1.3 million) to a nonprofit educational station, WFIL Radio and Television moved its studios from a deteriorating Negro neighborhood in West Philadelphia to a spanking-new, ultramodern circular behemoth set on four acres of the most expensive ground in the area, a plot on City Line Avenue that borders the fastest-growing suburban complex in the country. The circular design provides full view and control of all the studios from a production center in the hub of the building. Almost every piece of equipment was custom built for the new facility, including a computerized programming unit that automatically operates video and audio sources on split-second schedules. The entire WFIL facility, the flagship of Annenberg's Radio and Television Division, is reportedly worth close to $10 million. When Walter Annenberg wants to go first class, he doesn't pinch pennies. (Yet, strangely, there is a marked contrast between his willingness to spend money on his broadcast division and his frugality in the operation of his newspapers, which will be detailed later.)

When Annenberg acquired WFIL, he also got the station's general manager, Roger W. Clipp. As it turned out, he alone was worth the price of the station. A fiery, aggressive pusher, the Napoleonic Clipp became Annenberg's field commander in staking out and capturing new outlets for the Triangle fold. In 1955 it got its Binghamton, New York, stations; its outlets in the Altoona-Johnstown, Pennsylvania, and Hartford–New Haven markets in 1956; its UHF station in the Lancaster-Lebanon, Pennsylvania, area and its Fresno outlets in 1959.

The broadcasting business is one of the most profitable in the world. Television stations can bring in at least 100 percent returns on their tangible investments year after year. Walter Annenberg's Radio and Television Division brings in one of the highest percentages of return in the business.

o o o

*Question:* How does a man like Walter Annenberg oversee the operations of such an immense, multifaceted corporation as Triangle?

*Answer:* Very closely.

"I work at my business," he once said. "I am in touch with every phase of it." And, he added, the fact that he would be in England assuming an additional duty would not mean that he would be substantially less active in it. London, after all, is not much farther from Philadelphia than his winter home in Palm Springs, and no distance away at all by wire. He said he eventually hopes to establish a separate private business office in London, which may be a precedent that will raise some diplomatic eyebrows. (Later, however, he told the Senate

Foreign Relations committee he would "abstain from editorial direction of his newspapers while in the diplomatic service.")

He is almost constantly on the telephone, probing, suggesting, conferring. The principal memory of him by a former associate is that of a man who would arrive every morning, stand over his open briefcase, and in windmill fashion throw to his subordinates a huge pile of memos and papers, work he had accomplished during the night. His mind works fast. He often jumps to conclusions in the middle of a report, very rarely ruminates long on a single subject.

He has a tremendous capacity for caring about minor details. An *Inquirer* employee who once was assigned the task of tying up Annenberg's Saturday mail and delivering it to his home in Wynnewood recalls that after a few weeks at the job he received a message from his superior: "Mr. Annenberg would like you to use less string."

The only encounter a former assistant to the editor at *TV Guide* ever had with Annenberg occurred one day when her boss was out of town. The president of Triangle happened to pass the office. He stopped, looked in, and wanted to know why, since the editor was away, the light in his office had to be on.

Annenberg has a consuming interest in every aspect of Triangle's operations. "You have the feeling that he sees you only in your relationship to your job," says one of his top executives. "Whether you're an elevator operator or a division head, the only thing that's important is how well you perform for Triangle. He has a strong, almost

Victorian sense of organization loyalty. He's the kind of guy who says things like, 'Does he wear our colors?' "

He can be the cold, callous businessman. At one conference not long ago a subordinate who had disagreed with his opinion mumbled unthinkingly, "Well, I may as well resign." Annenberg quickly shot back: "It's accepted." An unproductive ad salesman with a number of years with the firm was released just about a year before he was eligible for a pension. And some think the manner in which Annenberg forced out Roger Clipp, one of his very close associates and a key man in the hierarchy of the Triangle organization, is an indication of the uncompassionate fervor with which he directs the course of his empire.

Certainly one of the more revealing insights into Walter Annenberg's character emerges from the perspective of Roger Clipp's career. From the general managership of WFIL radio when it was bought by Triangle in 1945, Clipp rose to become one of only two vice-presidents Annenberg designated for his giant corporation. He and general counsel Joe First were the publisher's most influential advisers and only Clipp had the status of a true field general. In fact, it might even be contended that the credit for Triangle's fantastic growth and financial success over the years belongs mainly to Clipp. But, more significantly, the fact that Annenberg so long relied on a man like Clipp and permitted or demanded that he operate the way he did cannot be ignored in assessing Annenberg's own driving ambitions.

Roger Clipp was known by some of his employees as

the Iron Duke. An elfin-eared little man with a domed forehead, icy cold eyes, and sharp-edged jaw, Clipp was not the most beloved executive in the organization. He demanded a superior performance from both himself and his subordinates and often flew into a tantrum when he didn't get it. Not infrequently, he would take rather extreme measures to get his point across. One secretary remembers being away from her desk and rushing back to answer her long-ringing telephone only to be beaten to it by Clipp charging out of his office. Instead of answering the phone he angrily tore it from its socket. He once reported his own station manager at WFIL, George Koehler (who was later to succeed Clipp as division head), to the city fire marshal for maintaining a fire hazard on the building's loading dock. To punish a clerk who had neglected to lock the mail room one evening, he removed and hid every last piece of mail in the place. Dissatisfied one morning with the waxing and polishing job the night maintenance men had done, he called them from their homes and made them polish and repolish the station's floors the entire day. (That, for a while, earned him the nickname "Old Yellowstain" from some of his associates.)

Yet it was Roger Clipp's driving force that almost singlehandedly built the broadcasting end of Annenberg's empire. Year after year he produced higher percentages of profit than the rest of the industry. When *TV Guide* was being formulated, it was he who went around the country for Annenberg buying up local editions of TV listings. His life was devoted to Triangle.

Early in 1967, Clipp suffered a heart attack. He went
away for a while, rested, and returned in good shape to
his post. Soon, however, those close to him saw him turn
moody and irritable. It became obvious that his relationship with Annenberg had changed. Annenberg, in fact,
had told him that he wanted him to retire. Clipp re-
sisted, but Annenberg pulled out a mandatory age agree-
ment that he had gotten Clipp to sign eight months prior
"as a matter of form." Still Clipp balked, especially since
it appeared that his own choice as his successor wasn't
going to be selected.

Whether Annenberg was concerned for Clipp's health
or whether, as a former associate suggests, he was afraid
it would "look bad for Triangle" if Clipp died in office,
is not known. What is known is that Clipp flew to Florida
one Saturday for a week's vacation. On Monday morning
at ten o'clock he received a call from Annenberg. "I want
to read you a memo that is going to be read at a staff
meeting this afternoon," Annenberg coldly told him.

After twenty-three years with Triangle, it was all over
for Clipp. He was offered a position as a consultant and
an office was maintained for him, but Clipp didn't stay
around. He left quietly, no parties, no farewells. "I
thought the whole affair was handled rather shoddily,"
says a WFIL executive. Clipp himself is reportedly bitter:
"People always told me he was a malicious man," he has
told friends. "I should have listened to them."

Most of the top men at Triangle feel an intense competitive drive that emanates from Annenberg himself.
This pressure is especially heavy in the Radio and Tele-

vision Division, a field far more rivalrous than most. "This is a competitive business," George Koehler has said. "The word here is kill, kill, kill!" Koehler is Clipp's smooth, efficient successor as head of the division and should know what he is talking about. As soon as he stepped into his new slot he fired almost all the men who had rubbed him the wrong way down through the years, including the television sales manager of WFIL at a time when sales were at a record high.

It was Clipp, however, who was thought over the years to reflect the kind of drive that Annenberg demanded. The history of his division is spotted with the bodies of men who couldn't keep pace. Several years ago a Triangle advertising executive jumped from the fourteenth floor of a Philadelphia office building. A year later a promotion assistant had a nervous breakdown. The following year Clipp threw a tantrum with the general manager of another station. Within six weeks the man was demoted, fired three months later; he died of a heart attack shortly afterward. That same year the pressure put another station executive in a mental hospital for treatment for three months.

Walter Annenberg works hard and he demands that the men who work for him push themselves in the same way. "I think we felt more of a drive to run in fat corporate profits than other stations," says a former broadcast man. "And it came from the top. We all felt that Annenberg had this great urge to make a lot of money so he could turn it back to the community, give it to some school or some charity. It was as if he was trying to get something off his chest."

Unfortunately, in his overwhelming desire to push Triangle to ever greater fortune and success, Annenberg has not always been sensitive to the fact that it is possible to load a man with responsibility beyond his capacity. More than one Triangle exec has crumbled because of that. A man named Clyde Spitzner, for instance, who while station manager of WFIL-TV was also responsible for *all* division sales, which meant every one of Triangle's sixteen outlets, worked enough for six men. "This is going to kill me," he confided to friends while struggling to maintain his hectic pace. He was right. He eventually dropped dead, undoubtedly from overwork. (Division head George Koehler, however, disagrees: "Spitzner," he contends, "was an intense, volatile, excitable individual and often was, in his own mind, beset by problems which would likely never occur.") It was only coincidental, of course, that not long after Spitzner's death, *TV Guide* publisher James Quirk keeled over at Philadelphia's International Airport one Saturday while rushing for a plane. Despite the magazine's huge success, the fifty-seven-year-old Quirk felt it necessary to hustle around the country personally making more than 140 annual sales presentations himself.

No man, however, can drive another man beyond the point to which he is willing to be driven. If men have killed themselves for Walter Annenberg, it is certainly by their own choice, not his, and to imply otherwise would be a gross misrepresentation of his character.

Nevertheless, the point to be made is that most of his top-echelon employees *feel* a driving force emanating directly from the apex of Triangle, the striving for an elusive goal, as it were, and anxiously attempt to keep pace with the pervading beat.

Annenberg's direct manner, however, in his personal relationships with most of his subordinates, is for the most part a relaxed one. Much too active a man to really be casual, he is nevertheless breezy and, for the most part, easygoing. He is the sort of man who will occasionally use a phrase like "old chappy" without being cute or snide. Sometimes short or curt, he rarely blows up over business matters. He has called subordinates to apologize for bad decisions that he himself has made.

"He's an exceptionally fine individual. He's very gracious, very honorable and charitable and a hell of a businessman," says Al Warren, publisher of *Television Digest*, one of Triangle's few disastrous ventures. (Another: *Quick*, a pocket-sized fortnightly for which Annenberg paid Cowles Publishing $250,000 in 1953 and which folded within a year.) *Television Digest* is a high-priced weekly newsletter sold by subscription to industry insiders. Triangle paid a rumored $600,000 for it in 1958 and poured a lot into it trying to expand it. When losses got too high, Annenberg asked Warren, who had been chief of its Washington bureau, if he wanted to take it over, gratis. Warren did, cut its operations and staff back drastically, and went on to build it into a very profitable business.

o o o

*After waiting more than nine months for Walter Annenberg's answer to my second letter, I decided to write to Joseph First, his right-hand man and Triangle's general counsel. I detailed for First the previous correspondence I had had with Annenberg. I told him that I had asked Annenberg to at least sit down and discuss the project with me. "From his lack of reply to my second letter," I wrote, "I assume he has no intention of doing that. Nevertheless, I feel that he might be concerned about the factual accuracy of information that is going into the article concerning the corporate structure that is Triangle."*

*I therefore asked First if he would sit down and talk with me. "Your cooperation," I added, "would contribute, I'm sure, in a positive way toward the article."*

*Two days later I got a reply from First. "I think I would prefer to let the matter rest where it is," he said.*

∘ ∘ ∘

Though Annenberg keeps in very close touch with every facet of Triangle's operations, he is very rarely seen except by a very few of his top personnel. He has huge, sumptuous offices, equipped with all the luxuries, in both the WFIL building on City Line and the *TV Guide* building in Radnor, as well as reserved parking slots, but he hardly ever uses them. "In the six years I worked for Triangle," says a broadcast man who was among the top half-dozen in the division, "I saw Walter Annenberg three times."

Annenberg had worked almost exclusively out of the

twelfth floor of the Inquirer Building. He very infrequently ventured out into his empire, in recent years wasn't seen on the *Inquirer*'s fifth-floor newsroom more than a few times a year. In fact, to many employees the twelfth floor has come to be considered a sort of mysterious sanctum. The elevators in the lobby are marked "Local to 11" or "Local to 13." They stop at the twelfth floor only for a very select few. All others who might happen to be summoned to the editor and publisher's office have to go down to the lobby and get clearance for the trip from the elevator starter, who first checks by telephone with the twelfth. There is no other way to reach that floor. The inner stairwell stops at the eleventh floor, resumes again at the thirteenth.

With Annenberg on the twelfth floor was the general counsel of Triangle Publications and, with the departure of Clipp, its only vice-president, Joseph M. First. If Annenberg can be said to have an adviser, it is Joe First. The sixty-five-year-old lawyer came from what was then the law firm of Murdock, Paxson, Kalish and Treen (now former Mayor Richardson Dilworth's firm) in 1939 to work on Moses Annenberg's legal problems. He stayed on to guide the young Annenberg through the early years after his father died, has been with him ever since.

Someone who has worked closely with First calls him "a brilliant management genius." A short, soft-spoken man with an unimpressive demeanor and quiet personality, he exudes an unemotional rationality, the personification of cool intellect. It is First, according to one insider, who soothes Annenberg's impetuosities and advocates the more conservative business approaches. Internally, with some exceptions, Triangle is not a dynamically exciting corporation from a management point of view. Its top-level executive salaries are par or under, its fringe benefits nothing to get excited about. It has lost a few very good young men over the years. (One not long ago was Annenberg's own nephew, Don Kahn, a smart, bull-headed young man who bucked an experienced power player in the *Inquirer*'s production department and lost.) At any rate, they do not flock to Triangle from the Harvard Graduate School of Business Administration, and some feel that First, as much as Annenberg, is responsible for keeping it free of innovative management concepts. "Joe First is a no-panache guy," says a former Triangle exec. "He is a cautious, prudent, conservative, shrewd little man."

(First's influence with Annenberg stopped short, most of the time, of the *Inquirer*'s editorial operations. In fact, one must except Annenberg's relationship with the *Inquirer* when examining how he runs Triangle. The *Inquirer*, as one of his own staffers put it, carried an "emotional freight" that does not burden his other operations. In many ways, Walter Annenberg, president of Triangle Publications, Inc., is different from Walter Annenberg, editor and publisher of the Philadelphia *Inquirer*.)

∘ ∘ ∘

There are more than eight thousand employees of Triangle Publications and every one of them is unques-

tionably certain of this fact: Walter Annenberg is the
absolute ruler of the empire. Some would even attribute
an omniscience to him. Almost everyone knows *someone*,
forty-eight notches from the top of a division or a department, who has received a personal telephone call
from "the man on the twelfth floor," questioning him
about a particular detail, suggesting something or offer-
ing a brief word of praise. And Annenberg does have the
habit of picking up the telephone and plunging down
through the organizational chart to speak to whoever is
responsible for the detail that concerns him. (His concept of the company's organization chart, says one cynical
insider, is more of an inverted "T" than a triangle.)

However, the fact that Annenberg is seldom seen, that
there is this aura of mystery about his character and his
motivations, that he is not easily accessible, and that he
does, in effect, actually own the whole corporation results
in the belief that every order and direction given in Triangle *must* emanate from Annenberg himself. There
have undoubtedly been a good many ridiculous actions
perpetrated in his name and there certainly are a number
of corporate shibboleths for which he is supposed to be
responsible.

One truck driver, for instance, recalls that when working for the *Inquirer* he questioned some of the loading
procedures. He was told simply: "Annenberg wants it
done this way." And a promotion artist remembers once
being assigned the job of designing a billboard incorpo-
rating a football field. He did, making the football field
green. When he submitted it for approval he was asked

to change the color. He wanted to know why. The answer: "Walter says he doesn't like green." Later someone had the nerve to question Annenberg about it. "Oh, that," he laughed. "Must have been because last year I objected to that hideous shade of green they had on that billboard." His objection to one bilious tone became a "Walter doesn't like green" dictum. (Only a few of his top men, by the way, address him as "Walter." Mostly it's "Mr. A." Sometimes his wife calls him "Wally.")

No one really knows Annenberg because no one is really close to him, with perhaps the exception of Joe First. (Roger Clipp was also reportedly once very close to him, but it's doubtful that Clipp today would contend that he really knew Annenberg.) "He must be a lonely man," says a friend. "I don't think he has it in him to be at peace with himself." There are contradictions in every man's character, but Walter Annenberg seems to have more than most.

His public philanthropies, for instance, are supposed to be in marked contrast to his business frugalities. In fact, some of his employees feel he is downright cheap. It took years to get him to spend the money to air-condition the Inquirer Building; it wasn't until 1969 that reporters on one of the nation's major metropolitan newspapers worked in the modern atmosphere of air conditioning. Yet he can be personally generous. One editor with a retarded child has been the recipient of his concern. And, to show his gratitude for friends' kindnesses, Annenberg will often donate large sums to their favorite charities.

He has been callous and even impersonally cruel in some of his business dealings, but he regularly shows great kindness and great thoughtfulness and even a good deal of compassion. He still sends small remembrances on occasion to some of his prep-school teachers and when an acquaintance lost a son in Vietnam recently he called him every day for a couple of weeks, mostly from California, checking on how he felt and repeatedly asking if he could be of help in any way.

Sometimes his generosity is impulsive. For years, on his way to work each morning in his Cadillac limousine, Annenberg would see an old lame newspaper hustler limping out of the Inquirer Building with a pile of the morning edition under his arm to peddle on some street corner. One day Annenberg ordered one of his assistants to find out the man's name and to tell him that he didn't have to work any more. "Tell him I'll take care of him for life," said Annenberg, and thereby banished the sight of the unfortunate old man from his morning view.

When a *Daily News* reporter wrote a sympathetic piece defending an elevator operator in Philadelphia Traffic Court after former watchdog City Controller Alexander Hemphill had attacked him for having a shoe-shine business on the side (the man had twelve children to support), Annenberg wrote a note to the reporter praising him for the story. He also asked him to tell the *News*'s managing editor, Ray Hunt, to take fifty dollars out of petty cash ("charged to me personally") and give it to the man for "a few little gifts for his children." (Hunt, a hard-nosed old-timer, ignored the note.) In addition, when Hemphill later called on him to ask his support for the next election campaign, Annenberg refused to give it to him and called him "penny ante." (To this day Annenberg doesn't know that he was actually conned by one of his own reporters. To juice up the sympathetic angle, the enterprising journalist, faithful to the tabloid tradition of his newspaper, simply invented a few details to embellish the plight of the poor elevator operator. The man, contrary to what the story said, did not have twelve children. In fact, he wasn't even married.)

The point is that Annenberg is capable of strong emotional reaction. A close friend recalls him sitting in front of his television screen and crying uncontrollably on the day that President John Kennedy was shot in Texas. He later announced that he would pay off the mortgage on the house of the widow of Dallas policeman J. D. Tippit, who was shot to death just prior to the capture of Lee Harvey Oswald.

Most of the time, however, Annenberg does not reveal his emotions, even keeping his sense of humor to himself, among his business associates at any rate. He did, however, think it hilarious when, during a Republican convention, he made the *Inquirer*'s curmudgeonly old columnist John Cummings go shuffling around a Pennsylvania delegation function wearing a "Stop Stassen" button. And he went into fits of laughter at a news release which announced that a well-known local lawyer, noted for his sexual exploits, was going to give a speech

entitled "The Effects of Automation on the Legal Secretary."

Annenberg does, however, have the ability to manifest
just the right touch of light humor when the moment
calls for it. An associate recalls a dinner party at his
Wynnewood home, a rare business affair attended by
his top executives and Triangle's major advertisers. As
usual, he was an excellent host, warm and gracious. Then
one of his cronies decided to offer a toast to him. It was
silly and pompous and stilted. Annenberg rose to reply,
walked over to the French doors that looked out over the
lush expanse of his estate and said simply: "Gentlemen,
I want to thank you for permitting me to continue to
enjoy the standard of living to which I am accustomed."

Walter Annenberg *has* always lived well. He is in excellent condition for a man in his sixties, something of a
health fanatic, and very conscientious about regular exercise. There is a gym in the tower of the Inquirer Building, tennis and basketball courts and swimming pools
(one indoors) on his Wynnewood estate. He is a gourmet of sorts, but was reportedly delighted when teenage
idol Jerry Blavat not long ago brought him, hot from
South Philadelphia, some home-made Italian specialties.
(Years ago, a local press agent would attempt to in-
gratiate himself with Annenberg by buying Jewish pastry
in a Strawberry Mansion bakery, putting it in a greasy
old bag, and telling him his mother made it special for
him.)

An exceptionally meticulous man, immaculately

groomed, and, for the most part, given to button-down shirts and conservative-cut suits, Annenberg consciously attempts to reflect knowledgeable good taste. (His wife says he even helps select drapery fabrics.) Both of his homes are luxuriously adapted to their settings. His Main Line estate, called Inwood, features a sprawling white stucco classic Georgian manor set on some fifteen acres of sculptured woodlands in the Wynnewood section of Lower Merion. It is valued for tax purposes at $244,000. It is loaded with a fortune in eighteenth-century English furniture, French Impressionist paintings, and a couple of Wyeths.

His newly completed California home may be the most impressive built anywhere in a long time. Estimates of its cost go to $5 million. Set outside of Palm Springs, long the retreat of the wealthy and the famous, the main house sits on what was once a desert hilltop, now four hundred acres of sodded fairways and greens winding through forests of imported shrubs, trees, bushes, and a dozen small lakes. (Annenberg's golfing guests don't have to replace divots on his fairways, he simply has the areas re-sodded.) Surrounding the estate, to provide a moatlike perimeter of privacy, Annenberg has kept an additional 750 acres of desert untouched.

It took five years to build. Designed by Los Angeles architect Quincy Jones and decorated by former silent movie actor William Haines (star of *Alias Jimmy Valentine* and *The Adventures of Get-Rich-Quick Wallingford*), the home has elicited rave reviews from all those who have visited it. (Wealthy Ben Gimbel, a man who has been around, terms it "the most significant home I've ever seen." He was especially taken with the sunken, mirror-walled showers.) Richard Nixon stayed as a guest during the Republican Governors' Conference the month after his election, with Annenberg hosting a private dinner dance before the meeting opened. (It was then that Nixon offered him the ambassadorial post. It was also then that Vice-President Agnew made a speech attacking what he called the "executioner press," naming some publications he thought should be used "to cover the bottom of bird cages." He wasn't, of course, talking about any of the publications owned by his host.)

A monument to Annenberg's penchant for privacy, the palm-fringed estate is bordered by a six-foot chain-link fence, miles of barbed wire, and electronically operated gates manned by uniformed guards. Reporters were barred from entering during the Governors' Conference. Mrs. Annenberg told syndicated columnist Vera Glaser: "We want to keep it to ourselves a little longer."

The main house is a twenty-five-thousand-square-foot mansion, set a half-mile back through a winding, fountain-bordered road from the main gate. (A separate two-bedroom guest house is nearby.) It is in contemporary style, natural wood with white trim. Its peaked three-story central roof covers a hall, atrium, living and dining areas. The imported Italian marble floors were laid by imported Italian artisans. The interior is alive with trees and shrubs and original sculpture by Rodin, Brancusi, and Giacometti. The giant-sized furniture, upholstered in white and pastels, was all specially made. So were all the facilities in a pool room designed to be the exact replica of a movie set, the game room in a millionaire's mansion where Jackie Gleason played in *The Hustler*.

A couple of hundred miles up the California coast from Annenberg's Sunnyland—the name he has given his baronial retreat—four million visitors a year, in their colorful shirts and slacks, straw hats and hair rollers, pay three dollars each and walk on strips of protective nylon runners through a huge, twin-towered castle, its rich tapestries fading, its statuary cracking, its elegantly carved wooden ceiling infested with insects. William Randolph Hearst built San Simeon in the 1920's, a monument to his necrophobia. It cost millions. It took Hearst's sons, after he died in 1947, seven years to persuade the California State Park System to take it off their hands.

Perhaps if Walter Annenberg's motivations were better known, what he considers the priorities of life clearly discernible, the psychic forces that drive him unquestionably apparent, it might be worth speculating why a man pours huge sums of money, which in no way could be considered a fiscal investment with potential return (who would buy a *used* $5 million home?), into a material opulence that would satiate the most avaricious devourer of the good life. And at what point do the burdens of maintaining such opulence (it takes a full-time platoon of landscapers just to keep the grounds of Annenberg's Sunnyland in shape) outweigh the pleasures and enjoyment that can be derived from it?

There are a couple of superficially apparent reasons—

and they may be the only ones—why Annenberg built a
Shangri-la like Sunnyland. First of all, he wanted a nice
place to entertain his friends and his guests, one commensurate with his stature and his success, as well as
appropriate to theirs. (You can't roll out the old Castro
Convertible for the President of the United States.)
Secondly, his wife is a Californian and she likes the cli-
mate and the people.

Mrs. Leonore Annenberg is another manifest exhibit
of Walter Annenberg's good taste. A very attractive but
not flashily pretty blonde, she is the niece of the late
Hollywood mogul Harry Cohn (subject of a recent best-
selling biography by Bob Thomas called *King Cohn*).
Before she married Annenberg, her life had had its share
of hard knocks. Born in New York in 1918, she early
lost her parents and was raised by an aunt in California.
Two previous marriages ended on the rocks, including
one to Lewis Rosenstiel, the founder of Schenley Dis-
tillers and a man many years older than she. She has
two children, both women now, one from each of these
marriages.

She complements Annenberg nicely. She was once, in
the days of quieter fashions, on the best-dressed list and
is always noticeably appropriately attired for every occasion. She seems a very level-headed woman, reserved
but not shy, candid, open, and disarmingly honest. (After
her husband was named ambassador, she told an inter-
viewer: "It's a challenge. I've never had to think about
what I said or did before.")

There is a good deal of California in Leonore Annenberg's attitude and disposition. (She was graduated from Stanford University in 1940.) Rarely somber, she prefers the light and the airy. She decorated almost every one of the seventeen rooms in the Annenberg Wynnewood estate in some shade of pastel, saw to it that fresh flowers from their hothouse daily brightened all the tables. She is known as a gracious hostess and will often walk up to someone she doesn't know at a party with a smile and friendly, "Hello, I'm Lee Annenberg."

A convert to Christian Science, she is a socially aware woman, knowledgeable and interested in cultural and civic affairs. She is on the board of the Philadelphia Museum, the Philadelphia Symphony Orchestra, the Academy of Music, the Moore College of Art, as well as the World Affairs Council. It was she who reportedly pushed Annenberg into hiring away the Philadelphia *Bulletin's* very social society columnist Ruth Seltzer with a fat expense account. (It's so fat that it is given an entry separate from the *Inquirer's* other editorial expense accounts.) Annenberg was not overjoyed with the idea, still occasionally blows up at what he feels are too many obvious commercial plugs in her column.

The Annenbergs have been married since 1951. Walter Annenberg's first wife, Veronica Dunkleman, was the vivacious, dark-haired daughter of a wealthy Canadian manufacturer from Toronto. They were married in 1938, had a daughter in 1939 and a son in 1940, and were divorced in 1950. She charged that her husband was "disagreeable and disliked her family." She subsequently married an automobile dealer in Washington, D.C.

o o o

*I had received First's reply to my letter in the morning mail. A few hours later I received a telephone call from First himself.*

*"You received my cryptic letter this morning?" he asked.*

*Yes, I said, I had received his letter.*

*"Well," he said, "I want to get this thing off dead center, if it can be gotten off dead center."*

*"Fine," I said.*

*"Mr. Annenberg has no objection to seeing you. As a matter of fact, he's perfectly willing to see you. However, I think there ought to be a procedure acceptable to him, and to you, too. I think you ought to send him a list of questions you want to talk to him about and then I will arrange with both of you a mutually satisfactory time to sit down with him and get an answer to your questions."*

*"All right," I said.*

*"Mr. Annenberg has assured me that he's perfectly willing to sit down with you and answer your questions, with the right, of course, to tell you when there's something he doesn't want to answer. You know, you might ask him if he's beating his wife and he might not want to tell you."*

*"That's understandable," I told First, and thanked him for his efforts in arranging the interview.*

*"All I want to do is get it on the right track again,"
he said. "And it's on the right track again not because
of my part, but because Annenberg is perfectly willing
to do that. You should know that if he isn't willing to
do it, nobody is going to talk him into anything."*

∘ ∘ ∘

There is an apocryphal—in fact, highly spurious—story
that has circulated over the years in some Philadelphia
Jewish circles. This is the way it is told: A number of
years ago Walter Annenberg went before the Union
League in order to gain admission. The admittance board
asked him a series of questions, all of which Annenberg
answered with flying colors. Then they asked him his
religion. "Why, I'm Jewish," Annenberg replied. "Gosh,
we're sorry about that," says the head of the board, "but
our organization does not permit entrance to men of the
Jewish faith." So Walter Annenberg goes forth determined to change his image. He divorces his Jewish wife,
contributes to non-Jewish charities, builds a school for
an Ivy League college. He divests himself of all affiliation
with Jewish upbringing, heritage, custom, the very religion itself. Then comes the day. Annenberg once more
appears before the admittance board. Again they ask
him a series of questions which he passes with flying
colors. Then they ask him his religion. Annenberg takes
a deep breath, proudly surveys the WASP-ish faces of the
board members, exhales and then with overwhelming
self-assurance he proclaims: "I'm a *goy*."

There are many in his hometown who think that story

is a real thigh-slapper. Actually, it is indicative of the kind of attitude that has visited offense upon Walter Annenberg down through the years, and that has brought from him a sharp and sometimes vicious response.

Ever since he was thrust into his position of power at the death of his father, Annenberg has had to contend with a streak of resentment and jealousy that has embedded itself into certain elements of the community. The upper crust of Philadelphia Jewish society never did appreciate the fact that Moses Annenberg, a man who had made his money supplying racing information to gamblers, picked this town to intrude into in such a flamboyant way. Subsequently there have been those who felt that his son has downgraded his Jewish heritage in an effort to gain acceptance into Main Line society. This attitude was partially based on the fact that local Jewish fund-raising drives never could get as much out of Annenberg as they thought they should. Annenberg squelched a good deal of this feeling when, after the Israeli six-day war in 1967, he contributed $1 million, the largest single gift to a welfare appeal in Philadelphia history, through the local Federation of Jewish Agencies. Yet an FJA insider said: "I think he's trying to soothe his own conscience for having rejected his Jewishness all these years." Annenberg can't win.

On the other hand, because he isn't a WASP and because he is rich enough to engender a certain amount of envy, Annenberg has encountered a good deal of snide resentment from some of the Main Line element. An article on the Main Line in *Holiday* magazine in 1957 completely ignored the fact that Walter Annenberg was one of its wealthiest residents; it didn't even mention his name. Another piece in the same magazine in 1964 was not as circumspect; it quoted a Main Line dowager as claiming that Annenberg gained social acceptance by collecting paintings and supporting the Art Museum. Then, in a stinging backhand slap it added: "On the surface, Walter Annenberg might seem to have everything against him as far as society is concerned. He was born elsewhere; though he is not a practicing Jew, his forebears were; and his father, as a result of a dispute with the Internal Revenue Service, spent some time in jail ('But nobody talks about that.')."

That same *Holiday* article noted, of course, that the Annenbergs "are now considered 'one of the most popular couples on the Main Line. Nobody would turn down an invitation to their house.' " It didn't take note of the snobbery that the Annenbergs have had to buck down through the years, or of the fact that a popular organizer of debuts turned down a request to handle a party for their daughter because the family is not in the Social Register. Nor did it note that some of the same Main Liners who accept invitations to their home enjoy whispering about Annenberg behind his back and circulating little stories about how anxious he is to be so socially proper.

Elkins Wetherill, for instance, the very proper president of the Philadelphia-Baltimore Stock Exchange, tells one of Annenberg arriving at a Main Line party in a chauffeured limousine with a liveried footman while others, being as pretentiously unpretentious as only the very rich can be, came in their gray Chevrolets or Buicks or Mercuries. Wetherill says that before the evening was over Annenberg had sent his limousine and his footman away and was picked up in a Chevy. Wetherill would notice something like that, of course.

The point is that Annenberg has, to some extent, been pushed into a concern for acceptance and driven into an anxiety about doing "the proper thing." (Before he left on a trip abroad once he called a reporter who had spent some time in the country he was going to visit. He told him he had been invited to a party at a certain couple's home. "Are they socially acceptable?" he bluntly asked.) Despite the fact that he now hobnobs with the top strata of society and among the very best of the bluebloods (he reportedly took dancing lessons with socialite Edgar Scott, is a very close friend of Penn Central chairman Stuart Saunders), and sits on the board of very prestigious corporations, he has had to contend with some formidable prejudices. (As a matter of fact, he *had* applied for entrance into the Union League for some time. When he was finally accepted and was going to be the first Jew admitted, he withdrew his application. He says he discovered it required a pledge of allegiance to the Republican Party, which he considered an infringement on his right to be independent.)

The man who now struts through the glassy corridors of the American embassy in London, appearing confident and self-assured, an easy if not totally certain sense of authority about him, is not the same Walter Annenberg who years ago was forced to ascend, wary and suspicious, to the corporate throne in which his father had been crushed. He is a very different man. He is a man who has overcome stifling personal handicaps, heart-rending tragedy, and spirit-searing vilification. He is a man who has fought back, sometimes courageously, always vehemently, often viciously. He is a man who has come a long way.

o o o

Walter Hubert Annenberg was born at 1:30 P.M. on March 13, 1908, in a large but unpretentious brick home at 742 Jackson Street in Milwaukee. He was delivered by the family physician, Dr. A. W. Meyers. He was the sixth child of Sadie Annenberg, who would later bear three more, one dying as an infant. Of all the nine children, he was the only boy. The only son of Moses Annenberg.

Every Jewish family has a boss. The boss of the Annenberg family, absolutely without a doubt, was Moses Annenberg. He was a domineering but not tyrannical father, stern without bluster, vigorous but attentive. At the time of his son's birth he was running his own newspaper distribution agency in Milwaukee. He had started it on $1,500 of borrowed money. When he left that town thirteen years later, he was worth $2 million.

Walter Annenberg was twelve when the family moved to Great Neck, Long Island. His father had become the general circulation director for all of Hearst's publications. Young Walter was sent to an exclusive boys' prep,

the Peddie School at Hightstown, New Jersey, just outside of Trenton.

Peddie is the epitome of the Ivy League–styled prep,
before student revolutions changed all that. The boys
wear ties and jackets and white wool crew socks and are
spoken to of such things as values and integrity and
school spirit. Walter Annenberg says he spent five "very
wonderful" years there, one in the lower school and four
in the upper. He has, however, in a moment of nostalgia,
told a friend, "Prep schools are lonely places."

Peddie's 1927 yearbook shows a young Walter Annenberg, a handsome, square-jawed lad with black hair and
dark eyes. It says he was called "Annie." It lists his
activities as basketball, football, and track and, for two
years, head of the prom committee. ("They were the
only years it ever made a profit," Annenberg recalls
proudly.) For that feat he was voted the class's "Best
Business Man." There is, in the yearbook, no indication
of any extracurricular cultural or intellectual interests,
no social pursuits or journalistic leanings. (He was on
the staff of neither the yearbook itself nor the school
newspaper.)

Walter Annenberg was a very reserved, shy, and withdrawn young man. One of the reasons he remained
socially retarded for so many years was undoubtedly because of his physical handicaps. He was extremely sensitive about his withered right ear, through which he
cannot hear. That sensitivity remained with him in later
years and, to an extent, accounted for his infrequent

public appearances and his penchant for privacy. All Triangle photographers have standing orders not to shoot him from an angle that would reveal the deformed ear, and Annenberg himself is still careful about his positioning at public gatherings.

The ear may also have influenced the development of a very bad stutter in his younger years. It was so bad that for a long while it seemed uncorrectable, but with treatment by a psychologist and a good deal of determination, Annenberg eventually brought it under control. Determination was one thing he has always had a full measure of. A veteran *Inquirer* reporter recalls his telephone calls down to the newsroom in his younger years. Despite the fact that *w*'s are one of the difficult blocks for someone with a stuttering problem, Annenberg would, instead of just using his last name, insist on saying, "This is Walter," painfully repeating the first syllable until he got it out.

Such adversities produce an inner turmoil which does something to a man's character. Maybe it kills it a little bit, or it strengthens it, or it gives it an ingrained streak of stubbornness. Annenberg's character must certainly have been kneaded by these adversities and by the subsequent personal agonies he has suffered. In 1962, his son Roger, a *cum laude* graduate of Episcopal Academy, committed suicide in Bucks County at the age of twenty-two. His death was announced a week after it had occurred. A few years later, Annenberg's nephew, Robert Friede, was convicted of the narcotics death of his socialite girl friend Celeste Crenshaw. (New York newspapers took the opportunity to mention Annenberg's name prominently.)

However, if there is one single factor that has shaped Walter Annenberg's character and, indeed, given guiding direction to his life, it is the legend and legacy of Moses Annenberg.

No man so venerates the memory of his father.

No man is so haunted by it.

Down through the years, the two most painful aspects of Moses Annenberg's career have been repeatedly shoved into his son's face. One was that the old man had made most of his money in the shady racing-news business; the other that he went to jail for income tax evasion.

"They have been like a whip on my back," Walter Annenberg has said.

Many slashes have been deep and burning. A number of years after the incident, for instance, the IRS enforcement chief who handled his father's tax case wrote a book about his career, devoting a whole chapter to the Annenberg affair. Elmer Irey called his book *The Tax Dodgers,* and subtitled it *The Inside Story of the U.S. Treasury's War with America's Political and Underworld Hoodlums.* The book won't be found in the Philadelphia Library.

Because of the legacy of Moses Annenberg's racing affiliations, Walter Annenberg took a lot of the heat during the 1951 local political battles, when the *Inquirer* backed the Clark-Dilworth reform ticket. The Republican candidate for district attorney, Michael Foley, bitterly attacked Annenberg after the *Inquirer* had dug up the fact that he had been arrested for drunken driving in 1936. Foley charged that Annenberg had made a deal with the Kefauver Senate Crime Investigating Committee in return for his not being called to testify publicly before it. "I wonder if the reason was that the *Inquirer* had already agreed to support the Democratic candidates in this fall's election in return for a clean bill of health?" Foley slyly asked. He then charged that Annenberg, as publisher of racing publications, "editorially supports the very crimes he also condemns in the pages of the *Inquirer*. A strange personality for any newspaper publisher . . . the knight in shining newsprint on the one hand . . . and the tool of the most vicious, meanful and powerful gangsters in America on the other." As circuitous as the rationale and unsubstantiated as the charges were, Annenberg was still forced to deny them.

Over the years Walter Annenberg has had to contend with the type of notoriety that comes as a result of the family name's early association with the more unsavory aspects of the racing and gambling worlds. In 1950, the Republican candidate for mayor of New York City, a man named Edward Corsi, charged that convicted bigtime bookmaker Frank Erickson was using his cell in Rikers Island Penitentiary as a base in the maintaining of his illegal operations. He also charged that New York's Commissioner of Corrections knew about Erickson's operations and that he had conferred privately with the gambler a number of times—once, according to Corsi, in the company of "Mr. Annenberg of the racing paper interests."

By that time, Annenberg had pretty much established himself as an important community figure in Philadelphia and something of an influence in national political circles (he would soon be asked to head a nonpartisan citizens committee to help bring *both* national conventions to Philadelphia in 1952), and as unlikely as it was that he would even consider secretly ferrying himself out to a prison in the middle of New York's East River, regardless of *who* was there, he was again forced to publicly deny the charges against him.

In more ways than one, it has been very difficult for Walter Annenberg to forget his father's legacy.

The trustees of the University of Pennsylvania reportedly hesitated for years before accepting his millions for the M. L. Annenberg School of Communications, a graduate facility a university of its stature had long been lacking. It was only after the composition of the board of trustees had changed that the university condescended to take Annenberg money.

Shortly after Penn did accept Annenberg's offer to found a school in the name of his father, this "news item" appeared in the Philadelphia *Evening Bulletin:*

> Four or five persons believed to be former friends and associates of the late Al Capone are anxious to establish the "Al Capone Chair of Taxation" at the University of Pennsylvania.
>
> Isidor Ostroff, a Philadelphia lawyer, wrote to Dr. Gaylord P. Harnwell, president of Penn, saying that he had been approached by some people interested in establishing the chair in either the Wharton School

or the Law School, depending on the university's needs.

Ostroff said he had been asked to find out what the prerequisites for establishing the chair are "from the standpoint of money and other inducements which the university will require. . . ."

Ostroff, a 1927 graduate of Penn and a 1930 graduate of its Law School, said the group he represents apparently wants to "correct the impression" people have concerning Capone.

The group wants to "create an aura of respectability about a name that has been dragged through the mud," Ostroff said.

Isidor Ostroff was on the Pennsylvania legislative committee that investigated Moses Annenberg's racing-wire business in the 1930's. He says that Walter Annenberg never forgot that. When, twenty years later, Ostroff was representing a group that attempted to sell the suburban Philadelphia community of Upper Darby Township a $1.6 million incinerator deal, the *Inquirer* "exposed" it, called it a fraud, and, says Ostroff, smeared his name across its pages for months. (Ostroff later won a libel suit on behalf of the Upper Darby commissioners against the *Inquirer*.)

Such bitterness, almost self-regenerative and seemingly perpetuating, is part of the legacy of Moses L. Annenberg. And to glean but a hint of understanding of the son who preserves that legacy, it is necessary to delve into the entrancing saga that was Moe Annenberg's career.

It is necessary because one of the central factors in

Walter Annenberg's character is his deep acknowledgment that he started his climb to wealth, power, status, and social acceptance from the middle rung of the ladder and that it was his father who put him there. Moses Annenberg, his son will everlastingly remember, started from the very bottom.

o o o

*I submitted sixty-one questions for Walter Annenberg to answer. I considered them preliminary to a more detailed discussion with him. They were both general and specific, intimate questions about himself and every aspect of Triangle's operations. It would have been the most exhaustive interview he had ever submitted to.*

*A few days after I had sent the questions I received another letter from Joe First. He said Annenberg had received the questions. He concluded: "The amount of time it would take to cover such a broad spectrum is just not available."*

*I quickly wrote another letter to Annenberg. I told him I had been presumptuous in thinking he would have time for such an extensive interview and asked him for time enough to cover just some important areas. "With your pending appointment to the Court of St. James's," I wrote, "I feel the necessity to do an accurate and comprehensive piece multiplies because of the fact that, considering its proposed length and scope, it will undoubtedly be used as source material by future researchers both here and in Europe."*

*That, of course, was also being presumptuous but I thought it might help put the thing in a whole new light.*

*The next morning I got a telephone call from Walter Annenberg. He said he could spare twenty-five minutes with me that afternoon.*

∘ ∘ ∘

A lot of men have started from the bottom, but it would be difficult to get farther down, socially or economically, than the East Prussian village of Kalwischen, a tiny hamlet in the far northeastern corner of the German empire near the Russian border. That's where Moses Louis Annenberg was born on February 11, 1878. His father's name was Tobias, son of Israel. For many years it was just Tobias, until a Prussian census taker proclaimed he *had* to have a last name and called him Tobias-of-the-Hill. Thus he became Tobias Annenberg.

There were eight children in the Annenberg family (three others had died at birth) and to keep food in their mouths Tobias farmed and kept a small grocery store. It was a very small grocery store because there were only nine families in Kalwischen and all were desperately poor. The families had lived there for centuries, fortified in their poverty by a deeply religious contentment. Then in the latter years of the nineteenth century, winds of change began sweeping across Eastern Europe and word began reaching the peasants that there was gold in the streets of America. The great tide of immigration brought Tobias Annenberg to Chicago in 1882. The rest of his family, including seven-year-old Moses, joined him in 1885.

Tobias Annenberg worked as a peddler, had a small grocery store for a while, and then went into the junk business on the side. (His oldest son, Jacob, would continue in the latter and amass a small fortune.) By the time Moses was twelve, the Annenbergs had moved to a small three-story building on State Street. Their junk shop was on the ground floor and they lived—all ten of them—on the floor above.

Moe Annenberg worked in his younger years as a peddler with his father, but his first paying job was as a Western Union messenger boy. He also sold papers in the streets and swept out livery stables. Before he was eighteen, he was tending bar in a saloon on Chicago's tough South Side. In 1899 he married Sadie Cecilia Friedman, a quiet, red-haired nineteen-year-old girl from New York.

The year after Moses Annenberg's marriage, the single most significant event in the history of Chicago journalism occurred: William Randolph Hearst came charging into town with a new newspaper, the *American*.

Hearst came into Chicago with a trunk full of money and a reputation as a yellow journalist and no-holds-barred competitor. The famous battle between his *Journal* and Joseph Pulitzer's *World* in New York still stands as one of the most spirited and vicious in the annals of American newspapering. And his appearance in Chicago signaled the start of what was to become the bloodiest and most ruthless circulation war in the history of journalism anywhere.

Hearst started the *American* as part of a deal that would give Chicago a Democratic voice in time for the presidential election and himself the presidency of the National Association of Democratic Clubs. He got to be boss of the clubs but his candidate, William Jennings Bryan, lost the big one. Nevertheless, the *American* was soon waging a fierce circulation battle with the established Chicago press.

Max Annenberg, Moe's older brother, quit his job in the circulation department of the Chicago *Tribune* and went to work as a solicitor selling subscriptions for Hearst's new paper. A young man with tremendous energy and drive, Max moved up through the ranks and was soon made circulation manager of the *American*. Then he hired his brother Moe as a solicitor and he, too, moved quickly up through the ranks. When Hearst decided to complement his evening paper with a new morning paper, the *Examiner,* he made Moe its circulation manager.

Down through the years Max and Moe Annenberg have been credited with being responsible for and chief battle commanders of the bloody circulation wars that marked that era of Chicago journalism. In fact, some have even attributed the start of modern American gang warfare to them. That is a slight distortion of the facts.

Even before Hearst arrived in Chicago, the eight daily newspapers had waged an incessant battle among themselves for higher circulation. The street-corner newsboys were the key. At the time, each newsboy handled only one publisher's paper and fought with the others for favorite corners. Some papers organized their boys into brigades directed by field agents. When Hearst arrived on the scene the best boys and the best corners had long been pre-empted by his rivals. The only way Hearst could gain a foothold was to use muscle. A rough business became rougher. As agents struggled to keep their boys in line and get their papers on the newsstands first there were daily fistfights, broken bones, and wrecked stands. And each day as the circulation managers of Hearst's two new papers pushed for a bigger cut of the business, the battles became rougher. Moe himself later termed them "terrible."

However, it was only after Moe Annenberg had left the *Examiner* in 1906, following a quarrel with his brother, that the shooting started. What happened was that the Annenbergs had hired a group of tough-fisted agents to gain Hearst his foothold. They used muscle to persuade newsboys to take their papers and drop the competition's. When, in 1910, Hearst's chief rival, Colonel Robert McCormick, hired Max Annenberg away from the *American,* these tough-fisted agents went over to McCormick's *Tribune* with Max. Hearst's editorial boss, "Long Green" Andy Lawrence, then began hiring his own group of sluggers and it wasn't long before blood began to flow. The armed gangs roamed the streets, burned rival trucks, beat up drivers, broke jaws of newsboys who refused to take more papers than they could sell, and, eventually, began shooting at each other. During the course of the war more than two dozen men and boys were killed and scores seriously injured.

Moe Annenberg, meanwhile, had moved to Milwaukee in 1907. (Max was later promoted to the $150,000-a-year circulation post at the New York *Daily News*. He was killed in an auto crash in 1941.) Moe left Chicago to go into business for himself. He had noticed that while competitive newspapers fought fiercely for circulation among themselves in Chicago, in outlying cities they turned distribution over to a single agent. With Hearst's permission, he had handled a small agency in nearby Aurora while he was still circulation manager of the *Examiner*. It was a nice supplement to his sixty-dollar-a-week salary, but he eventually had to close it for lack of time and funds. However, when the Milwaukee agency became available he quit his job, pawned all the family's jewelry—$700 worth—and borrowed $800 at high interest to buy it. Soon the business was yielding him $150 a week and the Chicago publishers were so impressed with the job he was doing they asked him to take over agencies in other cities. Before he left Milwaukee he was controlling the distribution of all Chicago papers in the thirty major surrounding towns.

Moe Annenberg was, above all, a promoter and it was through his promotion ideas that he jacked up circulation of all the papers he distributed. His son Walter many years later recalled the one promotion that marked the turning point in his father's fortunes. "He asked my mother what was the one thing she was always running out of," he remembers. "She said teaspoons. That was it! My seven sisters and I sat and wrapped teaspoons in tissue paper and tied them in blue ribbons for readers. He must have sold millions of those spoons!"

The spoons had the state seals of Wisconsin and all the neighboring states on their handles. Moe had coupons printed in the newspapers, women clipped them and presented them at his newsstands, where they would receive the spoons at an attractively low price. The promotion went over so well that Moe soon interested newspapers in practically every state and in Canada. It was the first venture that gave him the capital to begin investing on a large scale.

And he did invest. He bought into a Milwaukee taxicab business and opened an agency for one of the early electric motorcars. He ran a string of restaurants, drugstores, bowling alleys, and pool halls. He put up and bought and sold a number of buildings, and before he left the town, wound up owning more than $3 million of its real estate.

Once Moe Annenberg was asked how he became a millionaire before he was thirty. "It is the difference," he said, "between the well-fed house dog and the hungry wolf. I had a large family and I had to hunt or starve. I learned how to hunt and I kept it up."

Moe Annenberg always loved a challenge. He would even, it seemed, go out of his way to pick a fight. He relished the very spirit of competition and thrived on the glory of a hard-won battle. Certainly that had to be one of the reasons why in 1917 Annenberg, a multimillion-

aire with more than enough business interests to keep
him occupied, accepted the job as publisher of a newspaper owned by Arthur Brisbane in Milwaukee.

Brisbane, a handsome dilettante, had made a fortune
himself working for Hearst. The shrewd tycoon had
hired him away from Pulitzer's *World,* where, in competition with Hearst's *Journal,* Brisbane had broken
new ground in yellow journalism. He had discovered
that not only were the masses immeasurably stimulated
by sex and scandal, they were at the same time infused
with a humble yearning to learn. So Brisbane became not
only Hearst's top editorial captain but also a columnist-
philosopher who preached the homely virtues and became
one of the popular writers of the time.

Moe Annenberg was one of Brisbane's most ardent
admirers. Enraptured by the columnist's pragmatic philosophy, he would daily read Brisbane's words of wisdom
to his children, convinced he was contributing an essential element to their education. No matter how much
money Moe Annenberg had, he would have thought it an
honor indeed to be asked to be associated with such a
fountainhead of knowledge.

Brisbane had actually bought three newspapers in
Milwaukee, but he had consolidated them into a single
operation before he turned the reins over to Annenberg.
As it turned out, it was the Annenberg touch that the
new newspaper needed to really get it moving. In no
time at all, he pushed circulation from 25,000 to 80,000.
In fact, he did such a good job of making the paper a

success that Brisbane wound up selling it to his boss—Hearst himself—at a fat profit.

Hearst kept Annenberg on as publisher for a year after the sale. Then one day he called him: "Milwaukee is too small for you," he told Moe. He said he wanted him to come to New York and take over the circulation of all his newspapers and magazines. Moe didn't need the fifty thousand dollars a year that Hearst offered—his income from his own businesses was many times larger than that —but it was a tremendous honor to sit on the inner council of the powerful Hearst empire. So in 1920 Moe Annenberg packed up his family and moved to New York to take the job.

Moe Annenberg had triumphed over poverty and lack of schooling. His audacity and courage had taken him up the ladder from the rough brawling world of Chicago's circulation wars, his sharp mind and keen business sense had earned him a fortune. So despite the glory and the honor of sitting at the right hand of one of the most influential men in the nation at that time, there was in Moe Annenberg something that kept him from being merely an employee. He always had to strike out on his own. He had a restless energy and a predatory spirit that pushed him from that South Chicago junk shop to the luxury of his Long Island estate. That's why it wasn't long after he had joined Hearst in New York that he began looking around for some action of his own. He found it in the *Racing Form* in 1922.

Racing has always been big business. What makes it

so is not the amount of money that a good horse can win in stake prizes or the profitability of breeding a fine animal for stud; it is the millions upon millions of dollars gambled on horse races annually. The huge bulk of that wagered money is bet illegally outside of the race tracks. It is not known whether Moe Annenberg had any hesitancy at all about getting into that aspect of the racing business that traditionally has been supervised and exploited by racketeers and inevitably involved police corruption and political payoffs, often gang warfare and even murder. It is known that when the *Racing Form* came to Annenberg's attention, he immediately spotted it as a winner.

The *Racing Form* had been started several years prior by a Chicago newspaperman named Frank Bruenell. He had figured out that *the* most important factor in the horse racing business was not the horses but information about them. This had previously been available only to track insiders or others who came across it in a haphazard way. The *Racing Form* made racing information, or "dope" as it was called, available to the public and to bettors outside the tracks. It daily listed the horses running that day, their histories and past performances. Bruenell started it in Chicago, opened a place in Buffalo, and then moved to New York, where his publication caught Annenberg's eye.

The times were ripe. The sounds of the prosperous Roaring Twenties were echoing in the era's vestibule. The racing business was coming back strong after the slack of the World War. Bookies were beginning to garner more and more customers, who, Moe Annenberg knew, would clamor for more and more racing information. So Annenberg got together with two other Hearst employees, Joe Bannon and Hugh Murray, and bought the *Racing Form* from Bruenell for $400,000. Years later, after branches and printing plants for the publication had been established in Toronto, Chicago, Miami, Cincinnati, Los Angeles, Houston, and Seattle, Annenberg paid more than $2 million to buy out his partners.

As soon as he got into the business, however, Annenberg saw even greater opportunities—and profit—in supplying racing dope. The *Racing Form* could provide it only on a daily basis, which was all right for those who went to the tracks or who bet with corner bookies. But at that time there were millions of other bettors who frequented what were called horse parlors, or bookie joints, who wanted their information by the minute, right up until and including the start of each race. There were often hundreds of these bookie joints in every major city and, although they were illegal, they operated with relative immunity because they were controlled largely by top racketeers with connections in city hall and the police force.

The reason for the popularity of these bookie joints was their method of operation. A gambler could place a bet on a horse right up until a few seconds before post time, just like at the track, and then, through a system of elaborate charts and loudspeakers, he could watch and listen to the progress of the race as it was being run. It was fun and excitement and the next best thing to being there. Annenberg, once he got into the business, saw that immediately. And he also immediately determined that the basic factor in the successful operation of these bookie joints was their wire connection to the race tracks.

Prior to that, however, Annenberg had fairly well tied up all the major printed elements of the racing information business. Besides the dailies like the *Racing Form,* the *Morning Telegraph,* and the *American Racing Record,* all of which wound up in the Annenberg fold, there were weeklies to disseminate all the rumors and behind-the-stable news, monthlies to supply digests and cumulative charts, and even annuals to feed the more studious gamblers' appetites.

But the big money was in supplying that information which kept the illegal racing business going as a daily enterprise. Off-track gamblers had to know what was happening between the time they had received their morning *Racing Form* and the start of a race. Horses could be scratched, jockeys replaced, weather conditions suddenly change. Anything could turn the odds upside down. That's why what were called "scratch sheets" were so important. They were published locally and printed twice daily, once in the morning and once in the afternoon just prior to post time. Yet, as late as the information provided by the scratch sheets, it still wasn't the hottest source of racing dope. Only the wire from the tracks would provide that.

A smart telegraph operator in Cincinnati had figured that out shortly after the turn of the century. His name was John Payne and he set up a small company to supply

racing information from a few nearby tracks to bookie
joints in and around Cincinnati. Payne might have continued undisturbed with his modest but profitable
operation if Chicago hadn't later become one of the
bloodiest battlegrounds in the war for control of the
illegal gambling business in the United States.

The man who was one of the major figures in this war
was Monte Tennes. It was he who, in an effort to drive
his two chief rivals out of business, sparked the gambling
wars which brought a reign of terror to Chicago in the
early twenties. Concluded the Chicago Crime Survey
of 1927: "The complete life history of one man, were
it known in every detail, would disclose practically all
there is to know about syndicated gambling as a phase of
organized crime in Chicago in the last twenty-five years.
That man is Monte Tennes."

Tennes was waging his war for control of the bookie
joints in old-fashioned shoot-'em-up style. Machine guns
barked, bombs exploded, weighted bodies splashed into
the lake. There were political investigations, outraged
cries for reform, and scandal aplenty. Then Tennes
learned of Payne's wire-service operation in Cincinnati
and suddenly realized he had a weapon for control of
the bookie joints none of his rivals could match. He paid
Payne three hundred dollars a day to supply all his
gambling parlors with wired racing information. His
rivals couldn't compete against that kind of service and
Tennes soon became the undisputed gambling tsar of
Chicago. He controlled every one of the city's more than
seven hundred bookie joints.

Monte Tennes was Moe Annenberg's first partner in the racing wire business. Tennes had organized something called the General News Bureau to plug into Payne's Cincinnati wire. That was his foothold. He shortly afterward forced Payne out of business and the General News Bureau became the direct supplier of all racing news. By the time Moe Annenberg came into the picture, Tennes, who was getting old and ready to retire, had consolidated the operation and set it on a firm foundation. Annenberg may have paid Tennes as much as $500,000 for a half-interest in the General News Bureau.

Not long after Tennes sold half of his wire service to Annenberg, he made a deal with a sporty character named John L. Lynch for forty of the remaining fifty shares. (He later sold the remaining ten shares to two of his nephews.) Lynch thus not only became a partner of Annenberg's, he also succeeded Tennes as Chicago's gambling tsar.

Lynch was a colorful guy. He ran a place that was called the Den of Immunity, a combination bar, pool hall, and bookie joint that seemed to be relatively free of the annoying occasional police raids other establishments had to endure. Another of Lynch's operations, the Sportsmen's Club, was named in the Chicago Crime Survey as a clearinghouse for police graft. Lynch himself achieved a measure of national notoriety in 1931 by being kidnapped by a couple of snatchers with more guts than brains. Annenberg offered a $25,000 reward for the return of his partner but the kidnappers wouldn't bite.

It was only after Al Capone himself interceded that they yielded, for a payoff of $75,000. They reportedly didn't get much of a chance to enjoy their windfall.

By the time Moe Annenberg acquired his interest in the General News Bureau there had sprung up a number of other wire services which also supplied information on a national level. In addition, there had come into being quite a few middle-man-type operations which, for a fee, plugged into the national wires and then resold the service to the local bookie joints in a particular area. Moe Annenberg never got into any business and remained very long satisfied with just a slice of it. His predatory instinct soon had him prowling about looking to devour both his big and his little competitors.

What happened to one of the last small independent services is an example of one of the ways Annenberg got to be the wire-service king. There were at the time more than a hundred bookie joints being serviced with racing news by Annenberg's General News Bureau, the Empire News Bureau, the National News Bureau, or the New York News Bureau. About thirty of them, however, were buying from a small local wire service run by a man named Alfred P. Kelly.

Kelly had been getting his news by plugging into the National News Bureau wire and then transmitting it to his customers, charging them between $20 and $30 a week *each* for the service. He paid National $40 a week for the right to plug in, thereby clearing about $800 a week profit.

Kelly's troubles began when Annenberg's General

News bought out National. He quickly switched his plug to the Empire News wire, which cost him $20 more a week. When General News also bought out Empire, Kelly had to pay an even fatter fee to keep his service in operation. Shortly afterward, however, he got a call from the local manager of General News, Patrick J. Burns. From now on, Burns told Kelly, General News would supply all of his customers directly and he could close up shop. If he didn't object, General News would hire him and pay him $100 a week.

Kelly thought it over and told Burns to go to hell. There then followed repeated offers and, finally, outright threats. Kelly still refused to turn over his business to Annenberg. Then one day Burns called Kelly and said, "We're turning the case over to Mickey Duffy."

Duffy (whose head eventually got ventilated by four bullets) was Pennsylvania's top gangster and a close associate of Al Capone's, but Kelly knew him well and couldn't believe his friend would turn against him and side with Annenberg. He agreed, however, to at least talk again with Burns. When he walked into Burns's office, sure enough, there was Mickey Duffy. Kelly signed away his business and went to work for Annenberg.

Sometimes, however, threats alone weren't enough. The Dallas, Texas, manager of a tip sheet which competed against Annenberg's *Harvey A. Jr.*, a publication distributed through the South, testified later in a Chicago court that he had been beaten by Annenberg's hired thugs, taken for a ride, shot five times in the back, and left to die. A milkman found him along the highway and

saved his life. He refused, however, to return to Texas
to bring charges against his assailants.

Moe Annenberg could not, of course, be aware of all
the methods and tactics his underlings used in competing against rivals. Perhaps a few of them did occasionally get a bit overzealous in their work. All Annenberg did was map out the general strategy from his headquarters on South Dearborn Street in Chicago. There
alone his operation spread out over most of the block
and backed on a small entranceway through Plymouth
Court. It eventually came to be known as "Annenberg
Alley."

The question of whether Annenberg knew about or
approved of some of his employees' more rigorous competitive techniques must be viewed in terms of the man
he hired as the general manager of his entire operation.
James M. Ragen had been circulation manager of
Hearst's *Examiner* after Annenberg himself had moved
up. He was one of the toughest in the business, a man
with fists hardened in the Chicago stockyards and put to
use in the streets when Hearst first moved into that city.
Annenberg always liked him. In fact, when he eventually
was forced to step out of the wire-service business years
later, it was Ragen who somehow wound up with a piece
of something called Continental Press, the organization
which took over the job of supplying the nation's bookies
with racing information. (As might be assumed, there
eventually broke out a battle among the top racketeers
for the spoils of Annenberg's wire empire. Ragen was
killed in this "Wire Service War," as it was called, in

1946. A banana truck pulled alongside his car and a concealed machine gun opened fire. That didn't do the job, however, and while he was recovering in the hospital someone slipped a vial of mercury into his catheter. That did the job.)

One of the most interesting aspects of Annenberg's wire-service empire, however, was the fact that it not only depended on the existence of thousands of illegal bookie joints across the nation for its operation; it also very much needed the collaboration of one of the country's largest and so-called respectable business corporations, the American Telephone & Telegraph Company.

This is the way the system worked: At every track Annenberg had a staff of observers, clockers, handicappers, and other horse experts. They were constantly filing reports, rumors, tidbits, and the latest information designed to keep the atmosphere in the bookie joints charged with excitement. Then at post time they would give the odds and describe the race as it was run. All of this information went out on wires leased from A.T.&T. It was initially sent to Annenberg's News Bureau headquarters in Chicago, passed on to his various subsidiary wire services all over the country, then sent out to the bookie joints, some of which paid as high as four hundred a week for it. Although the system incorporated both telegraph and telephone, it was manned and operated entirely by Annenberg's men and not connected in any way with the public system. Only the wires and transmitting equipment were leased from A.T.&T.

When the wire services first began to flourish, A.T.&T.

was faced with the sticky question of whether or not it could lawfully lease its wires to such enterprises. Back in 1924 one of the company's own attorneys had written: "These applicants [General News Bureau and others] must know that a majority of their customers are bound to be owners of poolrooms and bookmakers. They cannot willfully blind themselves to these facts and, in fact, set up their ignorance of what everybody knows in order to co-operate with lawbreakers."

A.T.&T.'s top brass, however, put that opinion away in the company's safe and decided that they could not sit in judgment on the legality of their customers' businesses. Instead they came up with a new contract that turned out to be the key factor in the proliferation of the wire services. The contract simply stated that A.T.&T. reserved the right to cancel the service if at any time the proper public authorities declared it to be illegal.

It is not known to what extent the profit motive figured in this opinion, but the fact is that by the middle of the 1930's Moe Annenberg had become A.T.&T.'s fifth largest customer. By then he had bought or forced out of business more than two dozen competing racing wire services and was the sole supplier of information to countless thousands of bookie joints in 223 cities in 39 states. He was also the owner of every racing publication printed in the country, except for a few scratch sheets he permitted to compete against him.

He accomplished all this in a variety of fascinating ways, but one of his principal methods was to first buy

into an operation as a partner and then force out everyone else. That's what happened, for instance, to Joe
Bannon and Hugh Murray, his partners in the *Racing
Form*. Annenberg first bought control of its chief rival,
the *Morning Telegraph*, then went to Bannon and Murray and told them he wanted to buy them out also. When
they refused, he dropped the price of the *Telegraph* and
cut back his wire service to the *Form*. Since he had installed his own men to operate both papers, Annenberg
was, in effect, the manager, the referee, and the rigger
of the fight. Bannon and Murray began screaming, but
rather than watch their investment in the *Racing Form*
dwindle they finally sold out.

Annenberg tried to pull the same thing on his General
News Bureau partner, John Lynch, and that resulted in
the public revelation of another interesting Annenberg
business tactic.

What happened was that Annenberg organized the
Nationwide News Service to compete against the General
News Bureau. Since his close friend, James Ragen, was
the manager of the General News Bureau, it was not
difficult to switch customers from the wire service in
which he was a partner to the wire service he owned
outright. While Annenberg would lose money in the dis-
integration of the General News Bureau, he would lose
it to himself. Lynch, however, filed suit in the Circuit
Court of Cook County and in it he revealed Annenberg's
obsession with milking even the most minor aspects of the
racing-information business.

Lynch said that Annenberg had organized something

called the Universal Publishing Company to take over the printing of "rundown sheets" for bookie joints. Rundown sheets listed each race, the horses, jockeys, weights, morning odds, and other information. They were posted on the walls of the betting parlors to provide both the clerks and the customers with the facts about the day's races. Most bookie joints obtained them from local printers for about ten cents for a full set covering all the races of the day. Annenberg obviously saw that a monopoly on the printing and distribution of these sheets would be a little gold mine, there being *at least* fifteen thousand bookie joints supplied by his racing wire.

So Annenberg began printing rundown sheets, going around the country buying up small printing plants in the process. But his sheets didn't carry the names of horses, just numbers. Then he had his wire service and his corresponding telephone service (called "Teleflash") provide racing information and results in code numbers rather than names. Thus only those bookie joints who bought his rundown sheets would have the key to the numbers. His rundown sheets were, of course, five to six times more expensive than the uncoded ones.

What Lynch charged in his suit, however, was that Annenberg's company printing these rundown sheets was getting its information from the General News Bureau without paying for it. In fact, Lynch said, neither Annenberg nor manager Ragen ever told him of this arrangement. He claimed that Annenberg had, as a result of this secret deal, cleared a profit of more than $200,000 for four and a half years.

Annenberg's reply to Lynch's suit was legal audacity at its height. "It appears," his lawyers answered, "that on the face of the bill of complaint that the subject matter of the lawsuit is a division of profits made by supplying operators with certain essentials which are necessary in the conduct of said gambling or handbook business. Equity will not take jurisdiction of an accounting between participants in an illegal business."

Lynch was floored. Annenberg was claiming that the courts had no right to intervene in their dispute because they were *in an illegal business*. That may have been one reason Lynch capitulated. Perhaps there was another. Annenberg's general manager Ragen later testified that on the day Lynch quit, he, Ragen, delivered one thousand hundred-dollar bills to Frank ("The Enforcer") Nitti, Al Capone's top goon, for services rendered. Ragen didn't say what those services were. Lynch sold his interest in the General News Bureau to Annenberg for $750,000. At the time it was making a $1.5-million-a-year profit. Annenberg discontinued its operation and went on with Nationwide News Service as if nothing had happened.

∘ ∘ ∘

Moses Annenberg became one of the richest men in the United States. His annual income has been estimated to be as high as $6 million. He was the absolute tsar of the racing-information business, so much so that when one of his subordinates complained that a few small scratch sheets not in their domain were hurting the circulation of their racing papers, Annenberg could afford to be magnanimous:

"Besides," he wrote, "we simply cannot have everything, and like Mussolini when he started out to grab Ethiopia, he had to very carefully consider what he might be plunging into; but Mussolini had nothing to risk because Italy was on the bum and those who might have opposed his ambitions had, by far and away, much more to risk than Mussolini.

"Our position is similar to that of the English nation. We in the racing field own three-quarters of the globe and manage the balance. In other words, the few little nations that are left have to pay us tribute to continue. Now, why isn't that the most beautiful and most satisfactory position to be in which ought to satisfy even me?"

It was a good question, because Moses Annenberg wasn't satisfied. He was operating on the shady fringes of the underworld and he was sensitive about it. Later, when he got involved in Florida politics and some local politicians denounced him for his racing connections, he issued a statement which revealed just how sensitive.

He was, he explained in the statement, interested in wire and varied concerns. He admitted he owned stock in a corporation that in turn owned stock in some sixty or seventy corporations, some listed on the stock exchange, he pointed out. That corporation did also own stock in a company that, as he understood it, supplied racing and other sports news to newspapers and "others."

(Nationwide News Service, the racing wire, was indeed owned by something called the Cecilia Company, but Moses Annenberg was the only owner of the Cecilia Company, a holding entity named for his wife.)

At any rate, it was that sensitivity which perhaps led him one day, when he was lounging in his beautiful winter villa on Biscayne Bay in Miami Beach surrounded by rich neighbors who had made smaller fortunes in utterly respectable businesses, to listen to a suggestion that he ought to start another daily newspaper in the area. Perhaps. Of course, the fact that the mayor of Miami and his police chief had for years been waging a campaign to close the city's bookie joints, which were paying Annenberg close to $4,000 a week for wire service alone, may have also influenced him. So in 1934 he built a $300,000 printing plant and started the Miami *Tribune*. In a year he had a circulation of 100,000

As usual, the action started as soon as Annenberg stepped into the ring. Not only was he battling the rival newspapers, the *Herald* and the *News* (the latter owned by former Democratic presidential candidate James Cox), but he was also fighting the civic hypocrisy that tolerated the area's race tracks and swank gambling palaces where rich Northerners squandered their green but cursed with Southern evangelical fervor the bookie joints that catered to the home folk.

Following a 1935 grand jury investigation of gambling, Miami Mayor E. G. Sewell opened a campaign to close down the bookie joints, starting with a raid on the local headquarters of Nationwide News Service. Immediately, Annenberg's *Tribune,* edited by Paul Jeans, an old employee of the Nationwide News Service, wrapped itself in civic righteousness and began a free-swinging muck-raking campaign against Sewell and his public safety director, Sam McCreary. No leaf of their private lives was left unturned. Old skeletons were dragged from the closets and rattled on the front pages. "Whether the handbooks operate or not makes not a whit of difference to M. L. Annenberg and the *Tribune* as long as their operation does not involve the corruption of city officials and the police department," Moe proclaimed in an editorial spasm of civic decency.

The muckraking paid off. After digging up a bribery charge against Public Safety Director McCreary and getting him suspended, the *Tribune* pushed a slate of friendly commissioner candidates in the next election who won and voted Sewell out as mayor. The handbooks and bookie joints once again flourished all over Miami.

Despite the victory, Annenberg grew weary of the struggle. The *Tribune* was losing money and his editor, Paul Jeans, was killed in an automobile wreck. So when John S. Knight came along and offered to swap him his Massillon, Ohio, paper plus $600,000 for the *Tribune,* Annenberg took the deal. (Knight later also bought the Miami *Herald* and extinguished the *Tribune*.) In his front-page farewell editorial, Annenberg patted himself on the back for a job well done. He had saved the city of Miami from evil politicians and installed able men: "The city with its new commission is in good hands," he said. "Nothing remains but to go ahead."

A month after Annenberg left town, his new city officials were charged with shaking down the Florida Power and Light Company for $250,000. James Cox's Miami *News* led the fight for a recall election and the following year Annenberg's commissioners were swept from office and Sewell and his colleagues returned. The Miami *News* was given a Pulitzer Prize for its efforts.

Not long ago, the Philadelphia *Inquirer* produced, under the personal supervision of its publisher Walter Annenberg, a promotional booklet which detailed the history of that newspaper as well as the career of Moses Annenberg.

This is what it said:

> M. L. Annenberg started as a newsboy, vending Chicago newspapers on street corners, moved up into the circulation department of a Chicago newspaper, advanced from post to post, eventually acquiring, on his own, magazine and newspaper distributing agencies in a number of cities. After a long association with William Randolph Hearst, climaxed when he was named general circulation director of all Hearst newspapers and periodicals, Mr. Annenberg resigned in 1926 to devote all his energies to his personal enterprises.
>
> With his purchase of The Inquirer, that newspaper became his chief interest. He moved from New York to Philadelphia, and assumed personal direction of the newspaper. . . .

Ten years of Moe Annenberg's life—all that part of it which was consumed in making a tremendous fortune in the racing-information business—was deliberately omitted.

Walter Annenberg wishes those ten years never existed.

John T. Flynn, writing in *Collier's* magazine not long after Moe Annenberg purchased the *Inquirer*, said:

> Moe's real purpose was doubtless his desire to wrap himself in the heavily respectable pages of the old Philadelphia *Inquirer*, assume the role of spokesman for the rich and powerful of Philadelphia's Main Line, and thus bury the old scars and smears of the racing gambling news business under the heavy crust of conservative respectability. He would be Mr. Annenberg of the *Inquirer*—no longer Moe of the *Racing Form* and Nationwide News Service. And the *Inquirer* would be a monument for his son.

o o o

Walter Annenberg was twenty-eight years old when his father, shortly before selling out his Florida newspaper, bought the *Inquirer*. Behind the young man was an academically undistinguished career at an exclusive prep school in New Jersey, an even less distinguished performance at the University of Pennsylvania's Wharton School of Business which resulted in his completely dropping out after a year, and several years as an erstwhile dilettante but dutiful son who busied himself in minor capacities in his father's vast complex of racing information and publications. At the *Inquirer*, he was given a desk in a corner of his father's office and told to countersign checks in order to get an idea of where the money was going. He was also given the title of vice-president.

If Moe Annenberg did, indeed, buy the Philadelphia *Inquirer* as a legacy for his son, he couldn't have picked a newspaper that oozed more respectability. It was known as the "Bible of Pennsylvania Republicanism" and had always devoted itself to protecting the interests and expressing the views of Philadelphia's very blue-blooded society, those upper-crust Main Liners, the wealthy, removed, contented manipulators of the city's corrupt political structure.

The newspaper had had a dynamic history under James Elverson, who bought it in 1889, but when he died in 1911 it was inherited by his son, James Elverson, Jr., a playboy yachtsman with the honorary title of Colonel. It was this Elverson who built the huge white tower-topped $10-million Inquirer Building in 1925 on a rise of ground overlooking Philadelphia's City Hall. On its twelfth and thirteenth floors he created sumptuously appointed living quarters for himself and his wife and had them decorated with a fortune in paintings, including a $50,000 Corot. Colonel Elverson died in his beautiful apartment in 1929.

At that point, the *Inquirer* was granted in trust to Elverson's sister, the beautiful Eleanor Patenôtre. Once known as the "Pearl of Madrid," she had married the former French ambassador to the United States, Jules Patenôtre, and had taken up residence in Paris. Not particularly relishing the idea of returning to run a newspaper in Philadelphia, she sold it to Curtis-Martin Newspapers, which merged it with the *Public Ledger*. Payments, however, soon became faulty and it reverted to Mme. Patenôtre. Moe Annenberg bought the *Inquirer* from her in 1936. It reportedly cost him $15 million, of which $4 million was in cash and the rest in assumed obligations.

Annenberg may have bought the *Inquirer* to achieve a measure of respectability, but he certainly made no effort to go about it in a quiet way. Instead, he came upon the Philadelphia scene with his usual flamboyant determination to take control. One of the first things he did was to announce he was going to put Dave Stern's *Record*, the city's leading newspaper, out of business.

In his autobiography, *Memoirs of a Maverick Publisher*, Dave Stern claims that Annenberg tried to muscle in even before he arrived in Philadelphia. A suburban distributor was told, says Stern, that unless he sold out his business to an Annenberg agent from Chicago, he would lose his "franchise" to sell the *Inquirer*. With Annenberg in control of the distributors, the *Record*'s circulation could easily be curtailed, Stern reasoned, and immediately filed suit in court to prevent such tactics. At the hectic hearing, a young, ex-Marine of a lawyer named Richardson Dilworth put up such vehement battle on Moe Annenberg's behalf that he got himself fined for contempt of court. Stern won the case, but Annenberg was so impressed with Dilworth's truculent performance that he retained him as general counsel for the *Inquirer* at an annual fee of $50,000. Many years later, with the help of Walter Annenberg and his newspaper, Richardson Dilworth would become the fighting district attorney of Philadelphia, and then its mayor.

Dave Stern says that Dilworth's involvement with Moe Annenberg may have delayed his political career. He claims that he himself offered to back the young attorney long before he took his first step in politics, but Dilworth told him, "I can't afford to give up that retainer."

Dave Stern was a scrappy little newspaperman who had risen from cub reporter to journalistic entrepreneur. A member of Philadelphia's Jewish gentry (which may have also rankled the humbly born Annenberg), Stern acquired the *Record* from John Wanamaker, the giant Philadelphia retailing firm, in 1928 and pumped its circulation by employing a lot of good reporters and infusing them with an aggressive editorial spirit. His chief financial backer was real estate tycoon Albert M. Greenfield, a chunky-faced financial wizard whose Bankers Securities Corporation came to control a number of big retailing chains, including Bonwit Teller and Loft's Candy.

Besides his newspaper interests, however, Stern had also become deeply involved in politics, had been one of the "For Roosevelt Before Chicago" crowd (those who had backed FDR before the 1932 Democratic convention), was instrumental in installing Governor George Earle in Harrisburg, and was the major voice and defender of New Deal liberal ideas in the Republican stronghold that was Philadelphia.

The fact that he had been an ardent Democrat in Florida and that his Miami paper had editorially supported Roosevelt didn't adulterate in the least Moe Annenberg's eagerness to fervidly wave the Republican banner in Pennsylvania. In no time at all he was being mentioned along with Joe Pew and Joe Grundy as one of the triumvirate calling the shots in Pennsylvania Republican politics.

And, as usual, when Annenberg got into a fight he never pulled his punches. The preliminaries to the 1938 gubernatorial election became especially bitter, with the *Inquirer* firing one blistering barrage after another at the Democratic opposition, which included the candidate himself, Charles Alvin Jones, Governor Earle's "Little New Deal" administration in Harrisburg, Demo fat cat Albert Greenfield, the *Record*'s Dave Stern, and even Roosevelt himself.

It was an especially bitter campaign in which issues, and sometimes even candidates, got lost. Marveled *The New York Times:* "Much of the venom of the campaign has been directed not so much at the candidates themselves as at their backers. A visitor to this city during the last week or two might have reached the conclusion, judging from radio addresses and newspaper accounts, that it was a campaign between Mr. Annenberg, the *Inquirer*'s publisher, on the Republican ticket, and Albert M. Greenfield, Philadelphia real estate broker, as the Democratic nominee, with Mr. Pew and one or two others as Annenberg running mates and J. David Stern, publisher of *The Philadelphia Record*, and another Democrat or two running with Mr. Greenfield. . . ."

The Democrats, of course, didn't take Annenberg's broadsides lightly. Their counterattacks were just as bitter. Greenfield especially, after the *Inquirer* began dragging up stories that implied he pulled some fast deals in closing his Bankers Trust Company in 1930, fired back hard at Annenberg. In a particularly vitriolic radio broadcast, he branded Annenberg as a panderer to gamblers, using his ill-gotten millions to buy the *Inquirer* to cloak himself with respectability. He said Moe had been a strongarm man for Hearst and was responsible for the bloody gang warfare in Chicago. He charged that Annenberg was not satisfied with the clean competition the *Record* offered but that he was out to destroy its publisher, Dave Stern, and all opposition. In what has been called his rugged, biblical command of English, Greenfield described Annenberg as "a dog who had returned to its vomit."

Still Annenberg kept up his attacks. "Political skunks can wear themselves out directing their poison gas at me," he metaphorized, "but I shall continue to do my duty." And he did. As a matter of fact, so fierce and effective were the *Inquirer*'s barrages becoming, their concussions began to reach all the way to Washington. That's when Roosevelt himself sent his Secretary of the Interior, Harold Ickes, to Philadelphia to make his famous speech against Annenberg. It was a long speech, but the *Record* printed every word without one typographical error.

Said Ickes, in part: "I come to tell Pennsylvanians what I know about Moe Annenberg, the curse of two cities, because the prospect of turning the public contracts of Pennsylvania and the whole law enforcing machinery of this state over to a man of the record of Moe

Annenberg is the most alarming thing that has ever threatened my native state. For Moe comes from the world and from the lawless tradition commonly associated with Al Capone. . . ."

As the attacks on him became more frequent and more vicious, Annenberg took to assuming the mantle of martyrdom. He occasionally began to refer to the punches thrown at him as "blows below the belt." A former employee recalls coming upon him one evening reading an edition of the *Record* which was especially vitriolic in its charges against him. Annenberg shrugged resignedly. "It's the penalty of leadership," he said.

Name calling only seemed to help Annenberg where it counted: on the newsstands. He was doing what he said he would do, he was murdering Dave Stern and his *Record*. No one could beat Annenberg on promotion or circulation. He would even ride around with his truck drivers to make sure they were using the fastest routes and timing the lights right. He gave away twelve-dollar clocks with four-dollar subscriptions. With premium promotions, predated editions, and "jackrabbit" distribution, the *Inquirer* was being distributed from Maine to California. Every Sunday 30,000 copies were sold in Toronto. ("It didn't do Philadelphia advertisers much good," recalls a veteran of those days, "but it raised hell with the circulation figures.")

Neither did Annenberg neglect to inject the same spirit of hustle and aggressiveness into the *Inquirer*'s news-gathering methods. He may actually have gone too far, in fact, because the *Inquirer* began printing

court decisions before they were even handed down. At
one point, *Time* magazine noted: "For many months,
the *Inquirer*'s correct forecasts of Pennsylvania judicial
decisions had aroused the envious indignation of its less
astute competitors. Last week, when the Pennsylvania
Supreme Court handed down decisions on special session
bills dealing with an investigation of the State administration, it was not news. Ten hours earlier, under an
eight-column banner headline, the *Inquirer* had accu-
rately announced the court's action." (The Pittsburgh
*Press* later hailed the *Inquirer*'s "tip" as "a great ad for
Mr. Annenberg's racing publications," and suggested
that the racing-wire tsar "predict a daily double on the
Supreme Court.")

Nevertheless, the *Inquirer*'s rejuvenation under Moe
Annenberg soon caused Dave Stern to feel the pinch.
Annenberg's aggressive tactics were not only cutting
into the *Record* but also into Stern's profitable little
operation, the *Courier-Post*, across the Delaware River
in Camden, New Jersey. Annenberg had issued a South
Jersey edition of the *Inquirer* with complete news coverage in what had previously been the exclusive territory
of the *Courier-Post*. Using his vast financial resources
freely, Annenberg could and did put a larger staff of
reporters and photographers in the *Inquirer*'s Camden
office than the *Courier-Post* could muster on a double
shift. Thus Stern's earnings from his Camden paper were
quickly cut in half at the same time that his *Record*'s net
profits were reduced by a fat third. The pressure was definitely on the scrappy Dave Stern.

Many years later, Walter Annenberg himself would write:

> And thus began M. L. Annenberg's difficulties. *The Philadelphia Record,* with its close association with the Democratic administrations at Washington and Harrisburg, began to cry about a "circulation war"—the traditional term used by papers trying to preserve an entrenched position against a new competitor's product and sales effort that has become superior to its own—and enlisted the aid of the Federal Trade Commission (to investigate the adequacy of the *Inquirer*'s advertising rates), the FBI, State Police, the State Legislature and local authorities in a harassment of the *Inquirer* and its Publisher.

There is absolutely no doubt that the son lays the blame for his father's trouble directly on Dave Stern. But Stern declares: "I can truthfully say that I had nothing to do with it." He claims it was James Cox of the Miami *News,* whom Annenberg had embittered during his Florida battles, who brought the wrath of Franklin D. Roosevelt down on Moe. FDR had been Cox's running mate in the 1920 presidential campaign, but after Roosevelt was elected President in 1932, Cox, says Stern, ribbed him: "Franklin, you ought to be proud of the way you're pulling everyone back to prosperity—including Moe Annenberg. Under your administration he's making more money than Mellon and Rockefeller combined!"

Whoever did the pushing, it probably did not take a great deal of effort to get Roosevelt to start the wheels moving against Moe Annenberg. Despite his own obvious vulnerability to attack, Annenberg refused to lift the steady barrage of editorial fire thrown by his newspaper against the New Deal administration. In fact, he seemed to relish the idea of taking on the President. "Roosevelt figures the people are going to lose their form of government anyhow," he told a friend, "and so he thinks he might as well stay in as long as possible. He doesn't want his organization destroyed, because he wants to run again in 1940. He'll never get out until he's pushed out!"

Moe Annenberg could not quite comprehend that it was he, and not Roosevelt, who was heading into big trouble.

One of the first cracks in the Annenberg racing-information empire came as a result of a Pennsylvania legislative probe directed by former Philadelphia public safety director Lemuel Schofield as its counsel. He was a tough and merciless investigator who dragged out all the skeletons from the dark closets of Annenberg's wire business and finally got a law passed which prohibited wire services to bookie joints in Pennsylvania.

Then on August 11, 1939—a year after the legislative committee charged that Annenberg's racing wire was taking in $1 million *daily*—the big blow fell.

Moe Annenberg was indicted by a Federal grand jury in Chicago for evading $3,258,809.97 in income taxes between 1932 and 1936. (In 1932 alone, it charged, he paid only $308 of the $313,000 due.) Interest and penalties brought the bill to over $5.5 million, the largest in the Government's history.

Also indicted were two business associates and Walter Annenberg.

The IRS claimed that it had been checking Moe's books since 1935. It had not, it said, found Annenberg completely uncooperative. Later, Elmer Irey, then the chief of the Treasury's enforcement branch, recalled: "He offered us the use of a room in his office to check his records and then presented us with an oversize telephone booth in which to work and no records to work with."

Irey's agents spent years combing through a labyrinth of canceled checks, followed bookkeeping entries that disappeared into nowhere and confronted hundreds of reluctant witnesses. Annenberg did admit that there might be some irregularities in his records but only because his bookkeeping system had not kept pace with the growth of his business. "It is," he said, "the usual headache suffered by a leader in vast enterprises."

The agents kept digging, however, and eventually they began sniffing hints of fraud in Annenberg's records. False stock certificates and dummy stockholders appeared. They found erasures in books and minutes of meetings, payroll records for employees who never existed, payments of gambling debts written off as "political contributions." They also found a multitude of very questionable tax entries—such as listing the costs of his daughter's wedding at the Hotel Pierre in New York and Pullman cars to bring guests from Chicago as business expenses.

The IRS agents came up with most of this information, however, only after they had gotten a break as a result of a blunder by one of Annenberg's employees. One morning agent Nels Tessem, in charge of the crew combing through the racing king's records, walked into the tiny room that Annenberg had provided them in his Chicago offices. He was not in a good frame of mind. He was frustrated by not being able to plug the gaps in the case after working on it so long, and he was constantly irritated by the oppressiveness of the small room in which he had to work. And for some reason, on this particular morning, the damn place seemed even tighter. He kept a twenty-four-hour shift working in the room and he turned to one of the agents who had just finished up the night shift. "What's wrong with this dump today?" he asked. "It seems even smaller."

"It's probably those boxes in that corner," the agent pointed out. "They brought them in this morning."

Tessem took a close look at the boxes and almost screamed in delight. They were all Annenberg's private records, shipped from his palatial estate at Great Neck, Long Island, to his Chicago office. A messenger had delivered them to the right floor but the wrong room.

Following the IRS's opening blast against Annenberg, dozens of other charges followed, many of them indictments against a host of other business associates.

One of the charges was that Annenberg, a Philadelphia nightclub owner named Jack Lynch, a friend named Lou Simon, and an employee called "Chew Tobacco Pat" Burns had attempted to bribe a Philadelphia police detective who had been summoned to Chicago to testify about gangster Mickey Duffy's connection with the Annenberg enterprises. The detective, Clarence Ferguson, reported the attempt. Years later, when Walter Annenberg's close friend Sam Rosenberg became Philadelphia's public safety director, Ferguson was fired from the police force. He took his case to court and won, but he later apologized to Moe's son for testifying against his father. Thereafter, Ferguson's daring exploits as head of the Special Investigations Squad became regular fodder for *Official Detective*, which, by the way, used to be Moe Annenberg's very favorite of all the publications in his stable.

When trouble came to Annenberg, however, it came big. Not only did the IRS go after him personally as well as after his son; indictments were also handed down for tax evasion by many of the more than sixty-five corporate entities he controlled.

In addition, as a result of the clever scheme that gave him a monopoly on those number-coded rundown sheets used by bookie joints, Annenberg was indicted by a Chicago grand jury for running an illegal lottery.

Suddenly Moe Annenberg became fair game. The Pennsylvania Public Service Commission started an investigation of the telephone companies serving him. A bill for a further investigation of gambling and wire services was passed in the Pennsylvania legislature. Even Attorney General Earl Warren of California filed a suit in the courts there charging Annenberg and nine hundred bookmakers with unlawful conspiracy in distributing horse-race results. (Years later, Warren was Chief Justice of the United States Supreme Court when the son of the man he charged was sworn in as ambassador to England.)

On August 24, 1939, Moe Annenberg, a thin, gaunt figure in a gray suit and gold-rimmed spectacles, walked into the Federal Court House in Chicago to be finger-printed. He was accompanied by his son. It was the beginning of the end. The man who had lived in regal splendor in the Waldorf-Astoria in New York, the Warwick in Philadelphia, and in magnificent baronial estates at Kings Point, Long Island, Pike County, Pennsylvania, Miami Beach, Florida, and Sand Creek Canyon, Wyoming, seemed to sense that his next residence was destined to be within the gray walls of a prison. He issued a statement: "From the efforts and demands of the government agents, it appears that I may well paraphrase the words of Nathan Hale: My only regret is that I haven't enough remaining years to give to my country."

Back in the privacy of his offices, however, he was a little less restrained, angrily blaming Stern and Greenfield for his troubles. "I wrecked the New Deal in Pennsylvania," he said, "to show people how to get back to sound business principles of government and I'm going to be crucified for it. That's the kind of country we're living in."

Gloom settled over the Inquirer Building. Moe Annenberg, for all his flair and flamboyancy, was a very well liked boss who got along easily with his employees,

enjoyed occasionally rounding up the girls in the count-
ing room and taking them all down to Benny the Bum's,
where he slipped the orchestra leader a few bucks to
play "I'm Only a Bird in a Gilded Cage." In fact, Moe
Annenberg may have been the least disconsolate soul in
the building. His son was the one who seemed to be
taking it the hardest.

A former supplement editor recalls that one of Walter's
jobs was to select cartoons. He remembers bringing him
a stack of them one afternoon and the young Annenberg
being so dejected that he wouldn't even look at them.
"Take them away," he said. "How the hell can I laugh?"
Just then his father entered the room. He picked up the
cartoons and flipped through them. He stopped at one
and laughed. "Here," he said. "Print this one. It's funny
and it's the truth." The drawing showed two disheveled
scrubwomen down on their knees looking up from wash
pails at a couple of shapely females in fancy gowns, glittering with jewels and being escorted through the
mopped lobby by handsome men in tuxedoes. One scrub-
woman was saying to the other: "What did virtue ever
get us?"

At any rate, things just seemed to go from bad to worse
for Moe Annenberg. The U.S. Attorney General, Frank
Murphy, seemed adamant in prosecuting his case to the
fullest, wouldn't even listen to pleas from Annenberg's
friends and associates, who included some powerful local
politicians and high church dignitaries. Today Walter
Annenberg claims he has a letter from former Governor

George Earle, whom his father had vigorously opposed, which states: "President Roosevelt originally, personally told me that there would only be a civil suit in any differences existing between Mr. Annenberg and the Federal Government, and he emphasized this point. Later, under the constant needling of *The Philadelphia Record*, he reversed his stated position to me. I have always felt this action unjustified. This was, indeed, a terrible manifestation of what can be born out of commercial jealousy."

If Dave Stern's commercial motivations were behind Moe Annenberg's troubles, Annenberg would be damned if he would let Stern get the last grip. He kept the full details of his own income tax case on the front pages of the *Inquirer* and watched the circulation keep rising.

Well, almost all the full details. While the *Inquirer* dutifully noted the story of how Annenberg appeared in court one day and announced, as if in a token of penance, he was winding up the affairs of the Nationwide News Service and its subsidiaries, going out of the racing-wire business and thereby tossing away a $2-million-a-year bonanza, it didn't note that the Cook County district attorney had earlier notified the American Telephone & Telegraph Company that a grand jury had held that wire services to bookie joints were illegal, and that A.T.&T., which Annenberg had been paying close to $500,000 a year, had quickly pulled the plug out of every horse parlor in the country.

Annenberg finally decided not to fight the Federal case

against him. On June 6, 1940, he appeared in Chicago before Federal Judge James H. Wilkerson, the man who had sent Al Capone to prison, and pleaded guilty to one count of the many against him. A settlement had previously been reached. Annenberg had agreed to pay the Government $9.5 million in taxes, penalties, and future interest, over a seven-year period, with $1 million down and the Government taking security mortgages on all his properties except the *Inquirer*. As part of the settlement, it was agreed that all the other charges against fifteen of the associates and four corporate enterprises would be dropped. Among them were those against Walter Annenberg.

On July 1, 1940, despite pleas of ill health made for him by his lawyers, Moe Annenberg was sentenced to a three-year term in the Federal prison at Lewisburg, Pennsylvania. On July 22, after he was permitted to wrap up his affairs in Philadelphia, his son accompanied him back to Chicago for the sad trip to Lewisburg.

Moses L. Annenberg was No. 10197 at Lewisburg, but he was still listed on the masthead of the *Inquirer* as "chairman and publisher." And for a while he still took a firm hand in running the operation. He had each edition sent to him by express, combed through the columns with a discerning eye, and wrote out his orders in longhand for relay back to Philadelphia. He was still very much interested in every aspect of the newspaper business and when a new paper, the Chicago *Sun*, bowed

∘ ∘ ∘

in his old territory, he sent a young *Inquirer* reporter named Frank Brookhouser to do a series on it. And he was still very much the circulation man. His roar was heard back in Philadelphia when he discovered that *The New York Times* was being delivered to the prison three hours ahead of his own newspaper.

∘ ∘ ∘

Moe Annenberg was originally scheduled for parole on January 12, 1942. His son Walter had made several abortive attempts to get him out of jail, including intruding himself into the home of one of the members of the Federal Parole Board. He was unsuccessful until he contacted a political expediter named Carmon D'Agostino of the Renault Wine Company in New Jersey. D'Agostino, who was instrumental in arranging the parole of Atlantic City racket boss "Nucky" Johnson, was a close friend of Hall Roosevelt, the President's brother-in-law, and often visited him at the Hyde Park estate. It was D'Agostino, a stumpy, cigar-chomping type, who had earlier warned Moe Annenberg that Roosevelt was going to move against him. It was then that Walter, as D'Agostino was leaving his father's office, told him to stick to minding the wine business. Nevertheless, when Walter came to him for help in getting his father out of jail, D'Agostino said he would pull all the strings he could. That's how Moe came to be scheduled for January release. At the last minute, however, word reached Dave Stern back in Philadelphia and he raised such a hue and

cry, both in his newspaper and with Roosevelt, that Annenberg's scheduled release was postponed.

Eventually, however, Moe Annenberg's health began
to deteriorate in prison and because of it he was finally
paroled on June 11, 1942. The next month, on July 20,
he died of a brain tumor.

∘ ∘ ∘

*The interview lasted almost exactly twenty-five min-
utes. At the end of that time Annenberg's secretary
came in and said that his next appointment was waiting
for him. He apologized for not being able to give me
more of his time. His voice is resonant, almost gruff, and
he speaks as if he were choosing his words very carefully
and deliberately, even in his casual comments. There is
a certain force about his personality, a sense of open
directness. He doesn't tend to philosophical bantering
or intellectual generalities. He seemed, for instance, to
prefer specific questions about Triangle's operations
rather than any attempt to elicit broader viewpoints on,
say, the responsibilities of mass communications. He is
not evasive. There is almost a back-slapping heartiness
to his manner, but not quite.*

*As I was about to leave he said there was something he
wanted to show me. On a shelf behind his desk amid an
array of photographs of his family, his sisters, his mother
and his father, was a foot-long mahogany-and-bronze
plaque with an engraved inscription. "The words are
from a prayer," Annenberg said, reaching into a side*

drawer of his desk and pulling out a small, soft-covered blue booklet. "It's in here." He flipped through the pages and showed me the passage from which the inscription was taken. "This prayer book comes from the mausoleum in New York where my mother and father are buried." He turned and looked at the plaque for a moment. "I think the words are very appropriate. I have tried to live my life according to their dictates."

The words on the plaque are: "Cause my works on earth to reflect honor on my father's memory."

o o o

# PART TWO

# THE PRESS
# LORD

And now the story of Walter Annenberg begins.

It begins with a son watching his father—a proud, spirited man who had pushed his way up from a South Side Chicago junk shop to become one of the richest men in the nation—being besieged and broken by his political and business enemies.

It begins with a sheltered, withdrawn young man suffering the agony of seeing a loved one subjected to the public ignominy of arrest and imprisonment.

It begins with his watching helplessly as the elder Annenberg slowly withers within the steel-cold walls of a prison cell, a brain tumor smothering what was once one of the most brilliant and irrepressible of minds.

The story of Walter Annenberg begins with the death of Moses Annenberg.

o o o

*"Cause my works on earth to reflect honor on my father's memory."*

o o o

Walter Annenberg will never forget. The words on the plaque he kept behind his desk are more than just letters etched into a bronze plate. They symbolize an attitude he has attempted to ingrain within his own character. His impressive record as a philanthropist, his unflagging concern for what he considers the best interest of his community and his country, his personal generosity, his great contributions to cultural and educational institutions, and his innumerable positive efforts to be of service to his fellow man are all evidence that he has, indeed, attempted to dedicate his life to honoring his father's memory.

Further, he has taken his father's fiscal legacy and done an admirable and quite amazing job of building it into one of the great communications empires of the nation. The branches of Triangle Publications stretch their profitable way into dozens of fields, from magazine publishing through television to real estate, and set off the Annenberg name as one of the giants in the history of big business.

In view of that, it seems almost tragic that he failed to raise to distinction his father's most cherished legacy, the Philadelphia *Inquirer*. Especially so since it has been that newspaper which, by the very fact of his owning it, has given him the kind of personal status and power necessary for recognition in the leadership circles of the nation and the world.

Yet, in his stewardship of the *Inquirer*, he has repeatedly violated the canons of journalistic ethics by using the news columns of the newspaper for personal ends, employing them to further his own interests and ideas or to vent his spleen on those he opposes.

Most importantly, however, he has failed to establish the paper as an objective, reliable, and responsible channel of information.

Despite Walter Annenberg's personal efforts to implant himself as a major beneficent figure in Philadelphia, his handling of the *Inquirer* has tainted his reputation to the point where many consider him most basically an erratic, vindictive autocrat who often has acted, as one important civic leader put it, "in a rather berserk and bizarre manner."

Harsh though the judgment be, what Walter Annenberg made of the Philadelphia *Inquirer* does not reflect honor on the memory of Moses Annenberg.

Perhaps his failure here is a reflection of the fact that he is, after all, human, and it is not easy to hold onto the prep-school ideals of humility and courage and determined benevolence under the constant lashes of a community's unforgiving whip. Perhaps it would have been asking too much of the man to *always* abide by the tenets of the words on that plaque, to forever turn the other cheek, to ignore the slaps and slashes inflicted upon him for the sins of his father.

Unfortunately, Walter Annenberg, when he has slapped back, used the *Inquirer* as a weapon of retribution, thereby prostituting the paper's public responsibility. That is one of the reasons he failed to make it the newspaper it could be. Another reason is that he simply does not seem to know or understand the functions or obligations of a good newspaper.

Of course, there is nothing in his background that indicates that he should. There are no hints of a literary bent in his early years and no journalistic experiences during his school days. His formal education terminated at the end of a year of college and his initial roles in his father's sprawling organization were in various phases of its business operations. The *Inquirer* was therefore more a reflection of Annenberg's character than anything else, and that, in turn, is a strange amalgam of traits molded by a variety of forces, the principal one being the complex relationship with his father.

It was not an easy thing to step into the shoes of someone like Moe Annenberg. Self-doubts would have afflicted a man with the strongest of egos. For Walter Annenberg, a quiet, sensitive young man whose self-concept already bore the bruises of a physical deformity and a bad stutter, it was an awesome burden. And his father's martyrdom was itself a cross. Moe Annenberg had prostrated himself before the Federal Government and took the full dose of its vengeance in exchange for its dropping related tax-evasion charges against his son and

his other associates. Said Moe in announcing the settlement: "I want to do what's best for my son."

For many years Walter Annenberg kept in his office
a framed bunch of old coins, a few pieces of crumpled
currency, and a battered gold watch. He told visitors that
they were his father's complete inheritance from his
grandfather.

When Moses Annenberg died on July 20, 1942, his
personal property included about $55,000 in cash, two
Cadillacs, shares in Triangle Publications valued at $2.6
million, and five cases of Old Taylor whiskey valued at
$802. However, he also left his holding corporation, the
Cecilia Company, in trust to his son, with the stipulation
that his wife would get a third of the dividends from it
and Walter Annenberg the rest. The Cecilia Company
had held as many as seventy corporations, including all
his racing-information businesses, and once provided Moe
Annenberg with an annual income of more than $6
million.

Yet Walter Annenberg knew that of all his father's
assets bequeathed to him, the Philadelphia *Inquirer* was
his most revered possession. It was with this bastion of
conservative respectability that the elder Annenberg had
hoped to erase the old scars and stains of the gambling-
news business. It was also astride the *Inquirer* that his
father had ridden forth to do battle with the enemies who
eventually crushed him, so Walter Annenberg couldn't
help but feel a special dedication to continuing the
operation.

Walter Annenberg learned everything he knew about

the newspaper business from his father. Yet there's no doubt that if Moe Annenberg were running the *Inquirer* today, it would be a very different newspaper. Most obviously because there was such a contrast in temperament and character between father and son. The old man had a sense of flair and flamboyance, a lust for life and living. He would think nothing, for instance, of having Rosie Babos, the family cook, whip up one of his favorite Hungarian dishes, pack it in aluminum and dry ice, and ship it air express to him at his ranch in Wyoming, where he might be consumed in an all-night pinochle game with an old crony from Chicago. (That ranch, which cost half a million dollars, was one of the "business expenses" later contested by the Internal Revenue Service; another was a young lady named Gerty Boze, listed at $16,300 a year as a clocker for the *Daily Racing Form*. The IRS claimed she never performed any services for that publication.)

"Everybody who worked for the old man liked him," recalls an *Inquirer* veteran. "He was the kind of guy who made things hum, a man with a tremendous amount of enthusiasm for everything that interested him, from business to broads. He was always giving big parties and big bonuses." Moe Annenberg didn't give a damn about social distinctions. He often ate lunch in the *Inquirer* cafeteria with his truck drivers and his printers.

When Moe Annenberg ran the *Inquirer* he was the absolute boss, and although he eventually gave his son the title of vice-president, Walter's duties and responsibilities were limited. In fact, some recall the old man frequently disparaging his son in front of associates, blowing up at a mistake, or scoffing at a suggestion. "Walter had no aggressiveness at the time," remembers a staffer, "and Moe just didn't seem to take him seriously."

From the fabric of their style, character, and manner of living, it was hard to believe that father and son were cut from the same bolt. Emile Gauvreau, the first editor of the *Inquirer*'s Sunday supplement, recalled meeting the young Annenberg shortly after taking that job in 1937:

"Walter, as vice-president of the corporation, was acquiring some social prestige in the community. He was paying taxes in Philadelphia on a million dollars' worth of personal property. He lived the life of a gentleman bachelor, after a day's work retired to an apartment in the Rittenhouse Plaza described by its decorator, the noted Terrence Robsjohn-Gibbings, as 'Sans Epoque.' In Walter's vast living room, any books to be seen were beyond reach near the ceiling and bound in colored linen to harmonize with walls of beige. Draperies and fabrics on the furniture were native-spun in shades of beige and Tanagra pink. The library walls were bleached teakwood, the carpet of chrysoprase green. Above it all a gigantic, ancient Hindu-Chinese figure dominated the abode. Some said the bathroom had been turned into a Capri Villa with tub and washbasins of marble and bronze and all faucets with the heads of griffins. . . ."

In formulating those early issues of that new Sunday supplement, at that time called "Picture Parade," Gauvreau often found himself confronted by the contrast in editorial approaches suggested by father and son. For the first issue, for instance, Walter ordered a pictorial series on the world's great waterfalls, a picture in color of the Taj Mahal, and a spread on the birds of America by Audubon. He also wanted two pages of color photos of the glazed fruits in silver bowls and other delicacies of bright hues as served to the gourmet at the Warwick. When Moe heard about this he blew his top. "Audubon!" he shouted. "What the hell did he ever do for circulation? And pictures of food, with millions starving! Do you want to start a revolution?"

Moe substituted his own ideas for that first issue. One was a two-page photo spread of the butchering of a bullock by a rabbi, detailing every phase of the sacrificial ceremony, including close-ups of each deft slash of the *cholof* across the animal's jugular vein. Another was a page of pictures of a Zulu wedding in which the happy warrior stands his buxom bride against a tree and marries her by ceremoniously knocking out her teeth with his fist to show her how much he loves her. Another page revealed the festival ceremonies of cremation as they are celebrated in Bali and India. Two pages were devoted to the bloody duels of German students. Ten photographs explained the "Psychology of the Peeping Tom." A page entitled "Murderers in the Animal World" started off with the photo of a horned viper devouring a rat. And for those interested in modern sociology there was a spread on "A Day in the Life of an Advertising Model," starting, naturally, with her morning shower, and a series of pictures illustrating bad honeymoon manners and "how they can wreck your marriage at the threshold of happiness."

Yet as the issues progressed Walter kept insisting on his ideas of what the public wanted to read. Recalls Gauvreau: "Moe's son was interested in elaborate conceptions illustrating wealth. He liked pictures of millionaires who spent $30,000 a year to fly to work in Wall Street in $60,000 planes operated by $100-a-week pilots. Our supplement showed a number of these weary commuters landing at the Downtown Skyport in the East River in New York. It cost them a dollar a minute to reach their offices.

"My researches, under Walter's direction, also launched me into the fantastic fortunes of the Rajahs of India who live in splendor beyond imagination. Moe's son was familiar with the annual incomes of most of them, rattling off the figures at his fingers' ends, like a table of multiplication. We printed the pictures of all these princes of enchantment who were still alive, beginning with the Nizam of Hyderabad, who had an annual income of $33,823,097.

" 'Jesus!' Walter commented, while he studied a photograph of the turbaned gentleman. 'Have you figured up what that amounts to by the day? That's what I call money!' "

On the other hand, Moe Annenberg's editorial concepts were based on his long experience as a promotion and circulation man. He knew what would sell. It was probably for that reason, among others, that his stable of publications included some of the raunchier magazines then sold on newsstands. One, *Baltimore Brevities,* reportedly carried the scurrilous story about J. Edgar Hoover that caused the FBI chief to go after Moe with such enthusiasm later. Another, called *Click,* parlayed Moe's penchant for sensationalism to a 1.6-million circulation in two issues before it was banned in Canada. (A three-page photo spread detailing what a woman should do when in danger of being raped was typical of the type of features it ran. The caption on the last photo of that spread read: "Keep calm, don't run—but scream whenever you can.")

If anyone knew what would make a newspaper's circulation climb, it was Moe Annenberg, and he was not in the least modest about his own abilities. Shortly after he took over the *Inquirer* he issued an impressive promotional pamphlet entitled *The Story of the Philadelphia Inquirer and its Amazing Revitalization under the Magic Touch of a Dynamic Publisher—M. L. Annenberg.* Strongly commercially motivated, he nevertheless did a tremendous job in upgrading the newspaper's editorial quality. "You need ten men? Hire ten men," he told an editor the day after he bought the paper. Although he pushed daily circulation up from 280,000 to 370,000 and Sunday's up from 600,000 to over a million, Annenberg poured over $2 million into the *Inquirer* in the first few years he was running it. He hung little red tags on copy desk lamps reading, "Please turn off when not in use," yet when an underling suggested that one of his editorial ideas was too expensive, he would snap: "It's my money, isn't it?"

Still, Moe Annenberg's concept of what a newspaper should be was governed less by standards of quality journalism than by a "give 'em what they want" philosophy. Which is why shortly after he bought the *Inquirer* he began stuffing it with comics. By the end of his first year of ownership he proudly announced the paper would carry no fewer than fifty comic strips. A little later the *Inquirer* could boast that it had more comics "than any other newspaper on earth." Its Sunday edition was mummified with a wrapper of comics, the number "100" blaring in three-inch type on its cover, and readers came to approach newsstands with "Gimme the 'Old Hundred'!"

Nevertheless, at the heart of every good newspaper there must be a certain editorial integrity commensurate with its responsibilities. Considering some of the stuff that Moe Annenberg pulled, it is not irrelevant to wonder how much of the father's ideas about editorial integrity rubbed off on his son. As noted, Moe obviously saw no conflict in using his Miami newspaper to start a muckraking campaign against that city's mayor and police chief when they began raiding the bookie joints which were paying his wire service more than four thousand dollars a week. And when he came to Philadelphia and began embroiling himself in bitter political battles, he didn't hesitate to use the *Inquirer* to get in a few rabbit punches of his own.

One of the most blatant examples occurred during

Annenberg's feud with real-estate tycoon Albert M. Greenfield, a Democratic political rival and chief financial backer of the *Record,* the Republican *Inquirer's* morning competitor. The two millionaires had been at each other's throat for months, both enmeshed deeply in the gubernatorial campaign. Then Annenberg began having his reporters check into the circumstances surrounding the closing of Greenfield's bank, the Bankers Trust Company, following the crash of 1929. Finally one day the *Inquirer* proclaimed in a huge eight-column headline: GREENFIELD'S FIRM DREW $300,000 FROM BANKERS TRUST, LAWYER SAYS. The story quoted Philadelphia lawyer Dan Murphy's contention that a Greenfield company drew the money from the bank five days before it closed and implied that Greenfield did so knowing that the bank would fold. What the story didn't mention was that the transaction was merely a renewal of an old note. Greenfield sued, Annenberg countersued, and the whole thing was dropped after the political campaign ended, but the incident again revealed that Moe Annenberg was never averse to using the news columns of his paper to fight personal battles, whether politically or commercially motivated.

This matter of editorial integrity—the public responsibility of a newspaper to keep its news columns inviolate— is an important one, not only in relation to the quality of the *Inquirer* but also in attempting to understand something about the character of the man who made it what it became. Down through the years Walter Annenberg has, like his father, shown a willingness to compromise the editorial integrity of his newspaper in campaigns of questionable validity.

∘ ∘ ∘

One of the most interesting editorial campaigns, in terms of the distortion of basic questions involved, was Annenberg's successful crusade to open the Barnes Foundation art gallery to the public, especially since it revealed how the power of a big-city daily newspaper could be used to influence the opinions and actions of high-ranking government officials and even State Supreme Court justices.

The Barnes Foundation collection is housed in a twenty-three-room French Renaissance gallery (designed by architect Paul Cret) located on a large estate just outside of Philadelphia, in Merion. It is one of the world's most outstanding collections of art and art objects. Included among the more than 1,000 paintings are some 200 Renoirs, 75 Matisses, 35 Picassos, and more than 100 Cézannes. It is the legacy of Dr. Albert C. Barnes, a self-made man who built his fortune by manufacturing medicines and by concocting the formula for a compound called Argyrol, which, in pre-antibiotic days, helped to prevent infant blindness.

The Barnes Foundation was started as a tuition-free, nonprofit educational institution built on Barnes's theory of art appreciation. Basing his approach on the educational principles of William James and his friend John Dewey, Barnes felt that any man could acquire an appreciation of fine art by a systematic study of how artists use the basic elements of color, light, line, and space. The gallery was built as an adjunct to the foundation, an educational laboratory in which classes were to be held and students given the opportunity to use the master-pieces as study aids.

For many years that's the way it worked. The public was not allowed in the gallery because it would interfere with the foundation's educational mission. (Originally, Barnes did set aside two days a week for public visits to the gallery, but before it opened, a preview exhibit of what were then considered his daring and bold collection of Impressionists caused such a critical outcry it con-vinced Barnes that the general run of art patrons were snobs who didn't deserve to be admitted to his gallery.) Anyone could apply for admission to the foundation's free art-appreciation course, held in the gallery, and almost everyone was admitted in due time. Except the rich and the famous. Barnes was a rather eccentric fel-low who despised dilettantism and affectation, which he assumed were most associated with persons of inherited wealth, high social standing, or public celebrity. To these he reacted with a biting maliciousness that was often tempered with a touch of sardonic humor. When auto magnate Walter P. Chrysler, Jr., for instance, no mean art collector himself, wrote for permission to view "the magnificent group of pictures you have collected," Barnes—masquerading as "Peter Kelley, Secretary"—re-plied: "It is impossible at this time for me to show Dr. Barnes your letter . . . because he gave strict orders that he is not to be disturbed during his present strenuous

*In 1917 the Annenberg family consisted of Walter, his parents, and his seven sisters. Father Moe was then publishing the* Wisconsin News, *on the eve of the career which led to acquisition of the Philadelphia* Inquirer *as Walter Annenberg's special heritage in the honorable profession of newspaper publishing. Father and son—from a family group picture.*

WALTER HERBERT ANNENBERG AZ

Great Neck, Long Island

*"Annie."* College Intended: U. of Pennsylvania.

League Basketball (2, 3), League Football (2, 3), League Baseball (2, 3), Track Squad (4, 5, 6), Third Team Football (4, 5), Junior Prom Committee (5), Senior Prom Committee (6), Coach of League Football (6).

Entered Peddie, 1922.

*From the Peddie yearbook: Walter Annenberg, with the caption covering his nickname, college hope, and school activities.*

*April, 1940. Grim-faced Moses L. Annenberg, once head of a farflung empire of racing and other publication interests, strides into Federal Court in Chicago to plead guilty to charges of evading more than $5 million in income tax payments. He received a three-year sentence.*

*Moe Annenberg, publisher of the conservative Philadelphia* Inquirer, *confers with his executive editor, E. Z. Dimitman. Dimitman was a genius at following Moe's orders and guiding the capricious destinies of the* Inquirer.

*Walter H. Annenberg, photographed by Karsh of Ottawa, as he became a national figure, friend of politicians and international art dealers.*

*On the eve of departure for London, Walter H. Annenberg, ambassador-designate, visits President Nixon at the White House for an intimate chat.*

*On the way to Buckingham Palace by coach to present his letters of credence to Queen Elizabeth II, Ambassador Annenberg is escorted by the Marshal of the Diplomatic Corps. Soon afterward he played a widely discussed "bit part" in B.B.C.'s film "The Royal Family."*

*The Inquirer Tower, Philadelphia landmark, that now symbolizes the new ownership and management (Knight Newspapers) of the newspapers that the Ambassador suddenly sold, despite repeated denials, in late 1969, when circulation was sagging.*

efforts to break the world's record for goldfish swallowing."

Another incident concerned Barnes's run-in with the noted author and critic Alexander Woollcott, a fine dispenser of cyanide and syrup himself. Woollcott had come to Philadelphia as an actor in *The Man Who Came to Dinner* and, having rented a town house on Rittenhouse Square for the three-week stay of the play, he dispatched a collect telegram to Barnes asking to see the paintings. This was the reply he received:

"I was alone in the house this morning when a telegraph office employee telephoned that she had a telegram for Dr. Barnes, charges collect. I explained that our financial condition made it impossible for us to assume the additional responsibility and I declined to accept the telegram. She explained that it was from such an important man that I should call Dr. Barnes to the phone to take the message. . . . My reply was that Dr. Barnes was out on the lawn singing to the birds and that it would cost me my job if I should disturb him at his regular Sunday morning nature worship. The telegraph office girl is evidently a person either very sympathetic to my lowly station or an individual who knows that to thwart a man of your eminence would be flagrant *lèse majesté,* for she read the telegram to me. I write you thus, frankly, so that you will understand the dilemma I was in, and in the hope that you will forgive my not knowing what a distinguished person you are."

The letter was signed "Fidèle de Port-Manech, Secrétaire de Dr. Barnes." Woollcott could hardly have been expected to recognize the name. It belonged to Barnes's dog.

At another time, a titled European lady was visiting the United States and, having heard of the famous collection in Merion, wrote Dr. Barnes as soon as she got off the boat asking if she could stop by on her trip across the country and steal a peek at the paintings. Barnes's reply was very gracious. He said it saddened him to be obliged to tell Her Highness that on the very day she had requested to be admitted to the gallery an important charity affair was scheduled on the premises. The affair was to be an art exhibit of a somewhat different sort, he said, but he hesitated to explain the details. Oh well, he said, if Her Highness must know, it was to be a strip-tease contest for debutantes. He was distressed, of course, that he could not invite Her Highness to this event, but "out of consideration for the intrinsic modesty of the debs, it has been decided to limit the guests to the boy-friends of the contestants."

One thing is certain: Walter Annenberg didn't dare to mess with Dr. Barnes or his foundation while the fiery old eccentric was alive. Barnes was too scrappy a fellow, oblivious of notoriety and with a penchant for writing unprintable letters and using gutter language. There was nothing "proper" about Barnes; he had no respect for the Establishment and he was serious about nothing except his desire to give what he considered common folk an opportunity to appreciate fine art.

Annenberg and Barnes were two very different characters, types who would have naturally grated each other.

Annenberg also had an extensive collection of French Impressionist and Post-Impressionist paintings but there is no indication that he subscribed to Barnes's theories of art appreciation. Later some speculated that his wrath against Barnes was brought about by his being refused admission to the gallery, but there is no evidence of that and it seems unlikely that Annenberg, knowing Barnes's eccentricities, would even have requested it.

There are some, however, closely associated with the Barnes Foundation, who believe that one particular incident was a major factor in arousing Annenberg's ire. It occurred before Barnes died and it involved a critic named Henry Hart, a close friend and later biographer of the eccentric millionaire. Hart, who happened to be a former *Record* reporter, had been invited down from New York to lecture before a Philadelphia group called Friends of Art in Education. Barnes was the founder of the group and had arranged the talk himself. Hart, during the course of the lecture, began lamenting what he thought was the sad state of culture in Philadelphia. And at one point he reportedly said one couldn't expect much else in a town with a newspaper run by the son of a gangster from Chicago.

As soon as Albert Barnes died in an automobile accident in 1951 the *Inquirer* began splashing stories across its front page about a legal suit brought against the foundation by a taxpayer seeking to force it to open its gallery of paintings to the public. These "news" stories detailed the contention of a grieving art lover named Harold Wiegand. He claimed that since the foundation had been operating tax-free, it must be opened to the public. The paper backed up the prominent play it gave to these stories with indignant editorials asking why an "art gallery" given tax-free status should not be open to the public.

Two important things were deliberately ignored by the *Inquirer* in this initial barrage against the foundation. One was that the Supreme Court of Pennsylvania had many years before ruled that the foundation was not an art gallery *per se* but an educational institution and, like all schools, tax-exempt. Also ignored was the fact that Harold Wiegand was far from a disinterested party. He was the *Inquirer*'s top editorial writer.

Although Wiegand and the *Inquirer* lost their case in the State Supreme Court, Annenberg, with the help of the late Justice Michael Musmanno, achieved what he was after: the publicity and apparent posture of acting in the interests of the general public. The majority of the members of the Supreme Court dismissed the case on its legal merits, obviously taking note that there was no apparent public need and no spontaneous public clamor that necessitated reconsidering the basic premise of their earlier decision. But Justice Musmanno, in a flowery dissertation that was much longer than the majority opinion, dissented. And, as Philadelphia lawyer Gilbert Cantor put it in *The Barnes Foundation: Reality vs. Myth*, an excellent study of the legal machinations that followed, "the picture was quite different after Justice Musmanno presented the matter as a serious and wrongful denial of their substantive rights to the ordinary tax-paying citizens of Pennsylvania. His dissenting opinion was delivered not simply into published reports of legal opinions but also into the eager hot hands of what is probably the most powerful newspaper in the Commonwealth. The *Inquirer* already had a large financial and emotional investment in the case, which it would fight to redeem. Now Justice Musmanno had given the *Inquirer* the dramatic phraseology, the language of injustice, and the judicial authority with which to rally public opinion and support."

On that basis, the *Inquirer* maintained sporadic but bitter editorial fire against the foundation and, by pushing hard, eventually urged the Pennsylvania attorney general, then Anne X. Alpern, to take up its cause. Later Miss Alpern would admit that the State would not have entered the picture "were it not for the *Inquirer*." At the time, however, it appeared that the attorney general's office staff just happened to be browsing through some dusty old legal documents and just happened to find a technicality in the original charter of the Barnes Foundation that might provide a loophole that would get the *Inquirer* what it had long been after. Thus the attorney general filed a complaint against the foundation claiming that its charter stipulated that the gallery must be open to the public two days a week.

The trustees of the foundation answered the complaint and eventually the case that reached the State Supreme Court revolved around a very narrow question: Could the attorney general order the Barnes Foundation to produce its books and records in order to ascertain whether it was administering the trust in accordance with the provisions of the charter?

Editorial integrity would have called for the handling of news stories based on facts surrounding that question. In fact, even legitimate editorial comment should have addressed itself to it. The *Inquirer*, however, repeatedly played up the legally irrelevant question of tax exemption and the public's "right" to access to the gallery in its headlines and news coverage. It was aided and abetted in this attempt to cloud the real issue by Attorney General Alpern.

Whether Miss Alpern thought she was truly acting in the best public interest is not known. What is known is that not long after the Barnes case Attorney General Alpern, a Democrat, ran in an election for a State Supreme Court seat and the staunchly Republican *Inquirer* supported her.

The fact that Walter Annenberg's *Inquirer* took such a strong interest undoubtedly influenced the members of the State Supreme Court in the case before them. And none more than the late Justice Michael Musmanno. One of the most colorful judges ever to sit on the high bench, Musmanno was a brilliant jurist, a humanist and a progressive legal philosopher. He was also an egomaniac who loved to see his name in print and his words engraved for posterity. It was he who volunteered to write the Court's majority opinion in the Barnes case and, in so doing, crushed any hopes the foundation's trustees might have had to continue the battle.

Except for his conclusion, in which he noted that the

Court decided the attorney general did have the right to examine the foundation's records, Musmanno ignored the basic question and took up the *Inquirer*'s irrelevant alarum concerning the foundation's tax status. "If the Barnes art gallery is to be open only to a selected restricted few," wrote the eloquent jurist, "it is not a public institution and the Foundation is not entitled to tax exemption as a public charity. This proposition is incontestable."

The *Inquirer* splashed the decision large across its front page. The foundation's trustees, bowed and bloodied by both the powers of the Court and the press, gave up the fight and opened the gallery to casual visitors, thereby forcing the institution to curtail its educational activities. (The original Court decision upholding its tax-exempt status had envisioned just that, warning that "the unrestricted admission of the public would be as detrimental to the work of the Barnes Foundation as it would be to the work carried on in the laboratories and clinics of the University of Pennsylvania.")

A warm and close relationship between Justice Musmanno and Annenberg's *Inquirer* developed, largely as a result of his opinion in the Barnes case. He was an inveterate public speaker before civic groups, especially veterans' oragnizations, and the *Inquirer* never failed to give his pronouncements prominent play. Often the jurist himself would call the paper's newsroom from a little backwater town somewhere in Pennsylvania to dictate to a rewrite man the gist of his latest oration before some American Legion post.

It is not known whether Annenberg rationalized the *Inquirer's* vehement attack on the Barnes Foundation as eventually resulting in a service to the general public. However, not long after the gallery was opened, an interesting article somehow slipped into the Northwest edition of the newspaper. Written innocently enough by reporter Claire Huff, the article pointed out that no great crowds were rushing to view the priceless collection and that a visitor to the gallery would find it a thoroughly pleasant experience and be treated courteously by the friendly personnel of the foundation. When Annenberg saw the piece he blew his top and the next day there appeared in the "Letters to the Editor" column a short note attacking Miss Huff's article. The letter was signed "Art Major." Actually it was written by an *Inquirer* reporter, on orders.

That is not the only time an *Inquirer* reporter has been told specifically what to write. The feature article about the Main Line in the December 1964 issue of *Holiday,* which contained a backhanded slap at Annenberg ("On the surface, Walter Annenberg might seem to have everything against him as far as society is concerned . . ."), also aroused the publisher's wrath to the point of his interfering with the paper's legitimate news function.

It was coincidental that a few days after that issue hit the newsstands, four editors of *Holiday* suddenly quit as a result of internal politics. When word got out, *Inquirer* publisher's assistant Eli Zachary ("E.Z.") Dimitman, Annenberg's liaison between his twelfth-floor sanctuary and the fifth-floor newsroom, told a reporter to check out the story. "We want a rough piece," he said. "Mention how Curtis is falling apart." (At the time, *Holiday* was still one of Curtis Publishing's few profitable operations.)

The reporter called the *Holiday* offices and was told that the squabble would probably be patched over and the editors back at their desks after the weekend. The reporter knocked out a story which said exactly that. When Dimitman saw it, he said, "That's not the kind of piece we want." He then explained again the slant that he wanted taken and, in fact, he dictated the lead, or first paragraph, of the story. It ran in the following day's *Inquirer:* "The Curtis Publishing Co., long beset by huge financial losses, curtailment of advertising income, internal dissension, firings and dismissals, had a new headache Friday."

Dimitman obviously knew what Annenberg wanted because the implications of such an approach, on what was supposed to be a "news" story about an incident at *Holiday,* hit where it hurt the most, since Curtis was then scrambling to find investors willing to pull it out of its financial crisis. The *Inquirer* story, and a long series which subsequently followed it, was a rabbit punch to a company already on its knees.

o o o

What does a willingness to use his newspaper in such a manner reveal about the character of a man like Walter Annenberg? A number of things, of course, but it is especially relevant to his attitude toward his profession and, in turn, his public responsibility.

Walter Annenberg has always professed to be, first and foremost, a newspaperman. He says he was named after a noted Chicago front-page reporter, Walter Hubert Inman. When once questioned about his consuming interest in breaking events—he has wire-service machines installed in both his homes—he explained: "That's a normal curiosity of a newspaperman."

Yet, to most newspapermen, editorial integrity is the most sacrosanct of principles. It has nothing to do with the opinions, quirks, idiosyncrasies, private crusades, or personal political leanings the owner of a newspaper might validly display on an editorial page. It does have everything to do with the trust a reader has a right in a democratic society to place in a newspaper's unbiased presentation of the news. Editorial integrity to an honest newspaperman means that a paper's news columns must be unpolluted by nonjournalistic motivations, must be dedicated solely to the presentation of the truth without bias or prejudice of any sort.

It is the newspaperman's awareness that truth is such an evasive thing, a delicate and difficult balancing of the facts, that makes the concept that much more sacred. Critic Dwight MacDonald has written: "Facts are all very well but they have their little weaknesses. Americans often assume that Facts are solid, concrete (and discrete) objects like marbles, but they are very much not. Rather are they subtle essences, full of mystery and metaphysics, that change their color and shape, their meaning, according to the context in which they are presented. They must always be treated with skepticism, and the standard of judgment should be not how many Facts one can mobilize in support of a position but how skillfully one discriminates between them, how objectively one uses them to arrive at Truth, which is something different from, though not unrelated to, the Facts." Because a good newspaperman is inherently aware of this, because he knows that facts can be marshaled and presented in such a way as to distort, ignore, or deliberately conceal the truth, he considers any interference in his attempts to present the facts repugnant, however subtle or gentle or cloaked in noble motivations that interference may be.

An *Inquirer* reporter who was assigned to handle some of the Barnes Foundation stories recalls: "I found the first few pieces I did being completely rewritten by city editor Morrie Litman. I asked him about it and he said he was just making them 'more vigorous.' I got the idea and soon found myself looking around for things that would put the Foundation in a bad light."

That reporter has since resigned. There is something about the violation of editorial integrity that eats away at the professional soul of an honest newspaperman. Admits an *Inquirer* assistant editor: "I've worked for half a dozen papers in my twenty-seven years in the business, but I've never known one with such a ferocious turnover." The fact of the matter is that even among many who work for Annenberg there is a bitter contempt for the newspaper he published.

However, when a newspaper does tamper with its legitimate function to present the news objectively, it eventually reveals itself not only to those on the inside but to its readers as well. There are few among those Philadelphians who know what's going on, those politicians, lawyers, civic leaders, and communications specialists who comprise the core of the city's intellectual community, who had absolute faith in the *Inquirer*'s news presentation, who haven't at one time or other read a news story in it and thought, "I wonder what Walter Annenberg is up to now?" And even the paper's general readership has been shown to lack some faith. An independent research study done several years ago by a New York firm called Social Research, Inc., revealed reader reaction to its news presentation. It was so critical that Annenberg's underlings reportedly were afraid to even show it to him.

Yet if Walter Annenberg didn't know what many think of the *Inquirer,* it must certainly have struck him sharply and perhaps even painfully when the Harry Karafin affair blew up.

The case brought the *Inquirer* international notoriety. In addition, the manner in which the newspaper reacted to the crisis compounded the disgrace that resulted from the initial revelations.

Harry Karafin worked for the *Inquirer* for almost thirty years and was for much of that time its star investigative reporter. He was the best known and most feared newspaperman in the city. As a local insiders' gossip sheet later put it: "For years, lawyers cringed, city officials winced and politicians prayed when Harry Karafin walked into their offices. He broke more exclusives, triggered more 72-point streamers and spearheaded more journalistic crusades than any other newsman in the long history of the Philadelphia *Inquirer*."

Early in 1964, *Philadelphia Magazine* began checking into an organized ring of local racketeers who were raking in millions of dollars from a series of fraudulent business bankruptcies. The tremendous complexity of the ring's operations—controlled by top underworld kingpins through several echelons of fast-moving con men—had long kept it immune from criminal prosecution. In fact, when the magazine began its investigation the ring's existence was still considered classified information and very few people, outside of certain Federal and local law enforcement officials, knew the details of its illegal manipulations.

Among those who did know was the Philadelphia *Inquirer*'s award-winning veteran reporter, Harry Karafin.

Karafin had been a regular visitor to the bankruptcy courts during hearings for the firms involved in the frauds. Federal officials recalled that he questioned them frequently and appeared anxious to keep abreast of any new developments in their frustrating efforts to pin down the ring's illicit operations. In fact, one official even suggested that *Philadelphia Magazine* abandon its investigation because he knew that Harry Karafin had been working on the story for some time, was therefore far better acquainted with the details and was probably going to scoop the magazine with an exposé of the fraud ring in his daily newspaper.

But *Philadelphia Magazine* continued digging and

rushed the article about the fraudulent bankruptcy schemers into print. It appeared in its May 1964 issue. The article prodded the U.S. Attorney's office into stepping up its own investigation and subsequently prosecuting the ring's key operators, including the brilliant chief organizer, a six-hundred-pound hillock of a man named Sylvan Scolnick.

The editors of *Philadelphia Magazine* did not have to worry about being scooped on the story by the *Inquirer*. Harry Karafin never wrote a word about the bankruptcy-fraud ring.

It was that fact that initially aroused the suspicion of the magazine's editors about Harry Karafin. That and another interesting detail they had uncovered during the course of digging into the machinations of the bankruptcy-fraud ring.

The ring was an intricate affair with a variety of operations that kept multiplying and expanding. Explained simply, it would buy a small business with a good credit rating, order a huge amount of merchandise from manufacturers on that credit, sell it quickly out the back door at cut-rate prices, then have the front man who was running the business put it into bankruptcy, claiming he couldn't pay his suppliers because he had lost his money to loan sharks or bookies. Some businesses could con close to a million dollars' worth of merchandise from manufacturers before slipping into bankruptcy.

The ring eventually reached the point where it was juggling at one time more than a half-dozen businesses in various stages of the bankruptcy-fraud plan. In fact, a sort of headquarters had to be set up as a clearinghouse and control center for the millions of dollars' worth of merchandise being funneled through the ring's intricate network of buying and selling operations. A small respectable-looking storefront office on a small street in North Philadelphia became such a headquarters. It was given the name of Twin State Distributing Company, and it was, ostensibly, a home-remodeling and heating firm.

An extended surveillance of Twin State revealed that there was a variety of interesting characters frequenting the place besides ring boss Sylvan Scolnick and his various front men in the bankruptcy schemes. Among such characters were a number of racket-connected loan sharks, gamblers, dope pushers, bookies, strongarm hoods, and even a paroled murderer.

However, *the* most interesting character seen frequenting Twin State was *Inquirer* reporter Harry Karafin.

That, as it turned out, wasn't actually very strange. A check of corporate records revealed that Harry Karafin was the president of Twin State.

Thus did *Philadelphia Magazine* begin keeping a close eye on the activities of the *Inquirer*'s ace reporter. Finally, in its April 1967 issue, it revealed that Harry Karafin was a blackmailer. He had not only blackmailed bankruptcy-fraud boss Sylvan Scolnick, he had collaborated with him on other shakedowns.

Among the magazine's charges—later corroborated when Karafin was criminally convicted on forty bills of indictment—was that the reporter had used his position with the *Inquirer* to extort large sums of money, perhaps as much as $100,000 in one year, from dozens of individuals and corporations over a long period of time. He not only threatened to place unfavorable stories in the newspaper if he wasn't put on their payroll; in the case of several recalcitrant prospects he actually did it.

Although the *Inquirer*'s top editors knew that *Philadelphia Magazine* was investigating the activities of their ace reporter long prior to the exposé, it was only after Karafin filed suit against the magazine in an attempt to prevent publication of the article that managing editor John Gillen called the reporter to his office and fired him.

The readers of the *Inquirer*, however, were not told this. They were not told that the hundreds of Karafin-generated articles which they had accepted as legitimate news stories over the years were actually slanted, planted products of a corrupt reporter. The *Inquirer* kept the news of its firing its star staffer a secret for weeks. And although the incident was by any measure important news in Philadelphia, even the *Inquirer*'s afternoon rival, the *Bulletin*, forfeiting its competitive responsibility to staunchly maintain its long tradition of journalistic conservatism, genteelly ignored the sensational story. ("We feel it's an internal matter for the *Inquirer*," explained one of the *Bulletin*'s editors at the time. "Besides, the whole thing is very sad and damages all of us in the newspaper business.") Fortunately, most major publications outside of Philadelphia didn't think the archaic niceties of journalistic fraternalism should be given priority over their public responsibility. Because it was only after such publications as *Time, Newsweek, The New York Times,* the *Washington Post,* the *Los Angeles Times,* and others, immediately recognizing the national significance of the incident, sent reporters into Philadelphia to get the details of the story, that the *Inquirer* realized it couldn't sit on it any longer. (There had been nothing like it since the Chicago *Tribune*'s Jake Lingle was revealed to be on Al Capone's payroll.)

Finally, a month after it fired Karafin, the *Inquirer* did what no other newspaper in the history of American journalism ever did: publicly confessed that its top investigative reporter had prostituted his profession and the integrity of the newspaper as a "shakedown artist."

The Philadelphia *Inquirer* spread the story of Harry Karafin over ten full columns of its Sunday edition pages, pretending the facts had not been revealed elsewhere weeks before. Its headline: INQUIRER TRACES THE SORDID STORY OF ONE "REPORTER." The overline read, "With Sadness and Regret," but the story was deliberately written to convey a display of bitter anger and disgust.

Although the *Inquirer*'s "revelations" were an expansion of the charges made in *Philadelphia Magazine,* it repeatedly pointed out that Karafin was able to do what he did only by betraying his employers and being a "remarkably adept liar." However, it also admitted that a full explanation was demanded from Karafin only after he had filed suit against an unnamed "local magazine."

The implication was more than clear: If *Philadelphia*

*Magazine* had not undertaken an investigation of Harry Karafin, and if Karafin had not filed suit against the magazine to prevent publication of the article about him, he would still have been the *Inquirer*'s top investigative reporter.

Again and again the *Inquirer*'s story pointed out that Karafin carried on his activities without the knowledge of *any* superior or accomplice at the *Inquirer*. Yet, it admitted, he repeatedly and loudly claimed a close association with publisher Walter Annenberg and was able to squeeze large amounts of money out of people by effectively wielding the columns of the newspaper. He not only threatened to bludgeon recalcitrant prospects, he often *did*.

But, incredibly enough, said the *Inquirer,* it never received one valid complaint about the way Karafin was operating.

Were people afraid to report him to the *Inquirer*? Said the newspaper's own managing editor, Gillen: "I don't know what else to think."

If that were true, there is no sharper indictment of the way Walter Annenberg had run the *Inquirer* or a clearer revelation of the reputation of both his character and his newspaper.

The facts are obvious: Harry Karafin not only blackmailed those individuals and businesses operating on the fringes of legitimacy, sleazy fast-buck dealers who couldn't afford to complain; he also hit some large and powerful corporations, including First Pennsylvania, the largest bank in the city, and Broadway Maintenance

Corp., a national city service firm. And all silently capitulated to Karafin's demands.

*Why?* Because they *knew* Karafin would write unfavorably slanted stories that would appear in the *Inquirer*. They weren't afraid of Harry Karafin; they were afraid of Walter Annenberg's *Inquirer*.

John Reilley, former senior vice-president of First Pennsylvania Bank, later testified that Karafin was paid $1,000 a month for "protection" against distorted news stories that might embarrass the bank. No one at the bank ever thought of complaining to Karafin's editor and publisher, though Annenberg and a top bank officer were both members of another firm's board and met together regularly.

Melvin Rabin, the president of International Creditors Corp., a firm Karafin attempted but failed to blackmail, testified that the reporter told him he could get away with manipulating the news because he was in Walter Annenberg's will. Rabin, a husky ex-Marine, pointed out that he wasn't afraid of Karafin, but he was "scared to death" of the power of the *Inquirer*.

The point is not that Walter Annenberg was aware of Harry Karafin's activities, but that Karafin's victims all too readily believed that he was. When Harry Karafin told them, as he often did, that he was "Annenberg's hatchet man," the question that immediately came to their minds was not whether Walter Annenberg would have a hatchet man, but whether Harry Karafin was the anointed one.

That is saying something. That is saying something

about what people think of Walter Annenberg, despite his great charitable contributions, his enormous business success, and his impressive social achievements.

Harry Karafin was a product of the Philadelphia *Inquirer*. He never worked on any other newspaper. He was, in his way, one of its most loyal employees. When the Newspaper Guild struck the publication for thirty-eight days in 1958, he was among the first to cross the picket lines, claiming it was "the only course which will allow us to retain our honor as newspapermen."

Walter Annenberg didn't sow the evil seed that flowered within Karafin's distorted sense of journalistic morality, but he must be held responsible for creating the environment in which it so freely blossomed.

How could Harry Karafin have come to hold the concept of journalistic morality inviolate when down through the years he repeatedly watched it being abused by the man for whom he worked? Annenberg may very well have set out, upon the death of his father, to make the *Inquirer* one of the best newspapers in the nation. And, in fact, during those early years he steeled himself against adverse community reaction to Moe Annenberg's reputation and pushed the paper ahead with extended news coverage and a vigorous policy of civic involvement. But eventually his ideas of how a newspaper should be run, including the injection of his own interests into its news operation, led to a deterioration of its editorial quality.

◦ ◦ ◦

Walter Annenberg called himself the "editor" as well as publisher of the Philadelphia *Inquirer*. But he did very little editing. What he did do was undermine the legitimate handling of the news. In no way was this more apparent than in his refusal to permit the names of certain individuals to be printed in his newspaper, regardless of their inextricable association with any news event. Those who have made this blacklist—known uneuphemistically in the *Inquirer*'s city room as "Annenberg's shit list"—have inevitably done or said something to offend the publisher's sensibilities.

Ever-changing, the blacklist was not something that was officially posted in the *Inquirer* newsroom. Word was simply sent from the twelfth floor to the city desk, usually via the assistant to the publisher, E. Z. Dimitman, and thence down through the staff. Reporters, however, were usually never told specifically until they happened to write a story in which the blacklisted individual was involved. Former *Inquirer* columnist Rose DeWolf, for instance, once wrote a piece about the operations of the Philadelphia-Baltimore Stock Exchange, extensively quoting its president, Elkins Wetherill. When she turned it in she was told that Wetherill was on the blacklist and his name couldn't be used in the newspaper. She had to call Wetherill and ask his permission to attribute his quotes to an Exchange vice-president.

Wetherill, by the way, returned to Annenberg's good graces and was regularly featured on the *Inquirer*'s society pages. That was another feature of the blacklist: it was never static and names faded on and off regularly. A gutsy deskman would deliberately permit a name to slip through, especially if it had been on the list for some time, and, not getting a reaction from Annenberg, continue to permit it. And in many cases only Anneberg himself knew the reason for the editorial ostracism. It would be difficult to guess, for instance, what such entertainers as Imogene Coca, Zsa Zsa Gabor, or Dinah Shore did to arose Annenberg's ire. (His decree against Miss Shore even extended to *TV Guide,* which, at the time when her television program was near the top of the ratings, simply listed it as "Variety Show," omitting the name of its star.)

Another instance in which Annenberg's motivations were obscure involved Philadelphia's professional basketball team, the 76ers. Both the *Inquirer* and the *Daily News* were ordered to extensively curtail their coverage of the team, drop all features about its players, and not print any pregame information. Game coverage was confined to a simple formula: the 76ers got two paragraphs the day after the game if the team won, one paragraph if it lost. It became especially ludicrous to see the results of a Boston Celtics game splashed across the *Inquirer*'s sports pages while the local team's efforts were buried. Even the telecast listings were dropped, although Annenberg's WFIL-TV, by preblacklist contract, had to carry the games. Of course, all the promotional ads which the station usually ran were eliminated.

Eventually, the blackout began hurting the team at the box office. Although the power of the press probably wouldn't have helped a lousy team or hurt a good team, it proved devastating to the then mediocre 76ers. After a month of deliberate neglect by Annenberg's two newspapers, the team suffered an attendance drop from 4,000 to 1,600 average per game. In fact, the death knell for the 76ers might have sounded if Annenberg hadn't suddenly ordered his newspapers to end the blackout and resume fair coverage of the team. The reason for the publisher's actions was never made known. It may have had something to do with the rumored disagreement the owners of the 76ers had with Triangle, which controlled the sports arena in which some of the team's games were played. Too, he might have become aware of the publicity out-of-town newspapers, especially the big New York dailies, were giving to the fact that Philadelphia's basketball team was being ignored by its own hometown newspaper. One of the 76ers' owners, Ike Richman (who afterward suffered a fatal heart attack while cheering for his team) claimed he didn't really know what was behind Annenberg's display of power. He said that at one point he wrote to Annenberg asking why the team had been blacklisted. He never got an answer.

Such seeming capriciousness is frustrating from more than one viewpoint. There have been instances when some assistant editor on night duty faced with a late-breaking news story has had to spend valuable time frantically calling a superior to find out if a person involved in the story just *might* be on the blacklist. And it can be just as exasperating for the reporter out covering the story. One staffer recalls a particularly trying time when University of Pennsylvania president Gaylord

P. Harnwell was on the list. The *Inquirer* had been going through some fancy footwork to avoid mentioning his name in its news columns. The recipient of the prestigious Wharton School Alumni gold medal received it not from Harnwell but from an anonymous "university official." The guest of honor at a Penn Founder's Day luncheon was introduced by "a university spokesman." A significant letter to alumni calling for a comprehensive survey of athletics at Penn was written by "a high university official."

Finally things began getting sticky when members of the Penn chapter of the NAACP picketed Harnwell's office in College Hall demanding that the university not employ Jim Crow unions on campus building projects. Insiders wondered if the papers would be able to hold out under this sustained attack of a running hard news story. The answer came when an enterprising *Daily News* reporter sneaked into a faculty meeting and got exclusive quotes from Harnwell revealing how he would handle the pickets. Quickly the reporter knocked out the story and rushed it to his city editor. He was shocked to read, when the edition came out, that the impact of his exclusive succumbed to the priority of the blacklist. There was the ubiquitous "university official." Outraged, he demanded that his byline be taken off subsequent editions.

Again in Harnwell's case, Walter Annenberg's motivations were neither revealed nor apparent. There have been many instances, however, when the reasons for his blacklisting individuals have become known. Once while vacationing in France, for instance, he thought he was snubbed at a social function by an Iranian oil magnate named Nubar Gulbenkian. When he returned to Philadelphia Annenberg immediately ordered his staffers to begin digging up dirt on Gulbenkian. One reporter was sent to interview one of Gulbenkian's ex-butlers, who was living in the United States. Another was assigned to call the oil magnate long distance and to ask him how much he paid in income taxes. Gulbenkian, when he discovered what Annenberg was up to, merely laughed. He told the reporter who called him: "Send me tear sheets of what you write. I think nasty little men are funny when they pant and snort."

Another individual unfortunate enough to arouse Annenberg's ire was Philadelphia boxing promoter Herman Taylor. The dean of the nation's fight entrepreneurs, Taylor has put together more championship matches than any other promoter in the world, and his connections with the powerful men who control the boxing game are as strong as anyone's. Yet Taylor claims he was nearly knocked out of business when Annenberg's newspapers blackballed his fights after he had refused to increase the percentage that the Inquirer Charities was to receive from a match he had organized. And it wasn't only the blacklisting that hurt Taylor. Shortly after his disagreement with Annenberg, Triangle bought the West Philadelphia arena which Taylor used to rent for most of his bread-and-butter matches. The manager of the arena was told that from now on Taylor was to be kept out.

As a result of incurring Annenberg's wrath, Herman

Taylor says he could not promote a major boxing match in Philadelphia for over three years. Then one weekend Taylor was strolling along the Boardwalk in Atlantic City when he happened to meet an old friend, a woman who also was once a very close acquaintance of Moe Annenberg's. Over a few drinks Taylor told her of the troubles he was having with Moe's son. The woman listened, then got up and went to a telephone. When she returned she told Taylor, "You have a lunch date on Monday with Walter in his office." It was only after that conciliatory luncheon with Annenberg that Taylor got back into the publisher's good graces and again began promoting major matches. ("Hi, Herman!" Annenberg had greeted him warmly when Taylor stepped into his office. "How come you haven't been having any big cards lately?" Taylor bit his tongue and laughed.)

When nationally known consumer advocate Ralph Nader was a guest speaker in Philadelphia one evening, the *Inquirer* deliberately ignored his presence, and a column, written by an unknowing reporter, was killed. Walter Annenberg happens to be convinced that Nader is just a publicity hound undermining the capitalistic system by attacking such great American institutions as General Motors.

Annenberg has not been reluctant to consider himself something of a self-appointed protector of the Establishment and arbiter of its behavior. In fact, he has reacted strongly whenever he has disagreed with almost anyone's behavior. One day, for instance, he happened to see a wire-service photo of Carroll Rosenbloom, the owner of the Baltimore Colts football team, hosting President John F. Kennedy's father, Joseph Kennedy, aboard his yacht. Annenberg blew up in rage. Rosenbloom had just received highly unfavorable publicity by being sued by a man of questionable character, a gambler who was later deported from the Bahamas for being a "dangerous person." Annenberg thought Rosenbloom went beyond the bounds of propriety when, after being involved publicly with such a character, he had the nerve to taint the image of the President's father by inviting him aboard his yacht. He sent word to a reporter to dig into Rosenbloom's background and come up with an unfavorable article. The reporter, however, couldn't find enough dirt so, ignoring the facts, he produced a story so scurrilous it couldn't be printed. Annenberg's rage, as often happens, eventually died and the reporter wasn't told to try again.

Years ago, when builder Matt McCloskey owned the *Daily News,* he discovered he was on the blacklist and began playing games with the *Inquirer.* An active politician and civic leader, McCloskey attempted to involve or place himself at important functions in such a way that the newspaper couldn't avoid mentioning his presence. It repeatedly did, however, even cropping him out of photos when necessary. Finally one day McCloskey placed himself between two prominent politicians at a function in a photograph he knew the *Inquirer* had to use. "Let's see that s.o.b. crop me out of that one!" he gleefully told a friend. The next day the photograph appeared in the *Inquirer* and there between two prominent politicians was a gray blob. McCloskey had been airbrushed out.

Annenberg's blacklisting of McCloskey was reportedly inspired by the *Daily News*'s editorial campaign to help convicted holdup killer David Darcy avoid the death penalty. The *Inquirer* was vehemently fighting to send him to the chair. But Annenberg was particularly angered by what he considered to be McCloskey's tainted motives. Darcy happened to be the nephew of McCloskey's close associate and political secretary; and the millionaire builder and national financial chairman of the Democratic Party had earlier appeared on Darcy's behalf before the all-Democratic pardons board.

The McCloskey case again illustrates the chameleonic nature of the blacklist—and perhaps of Annenberg's character itself. Today both men are on friendly terms. "Personally," says McCloskey, "he couldn't be nicer. Every time I see him he acts like we're long-lost cousins." When President Kennedy named McCloskey ambassador to Ireland, Annenberg interceded with a Republican senator who was delaying the appointment. McCloskey contends he isn't aware of Annenberg's reason for blacklisting him. "I've often asked him," McCloskey says, "but he won't tell me."

Yet it is Walter Annenberg's motivations in consigning individuals to his blacklist that must be considered in any attempted assessment of his basic character. In discussing them with Annenberg himself, the impression one inevitably comes away with is that he doesn't quite understand why his motives should even be questioned. There is no arrogance in his attitude; merely a quiet, deep self-confidence in the validity of his own opinions.

o o o

Walter Annenberg's autocratic attitude manifested itself clearly in the *Inquirer*'s campaign against Democratic candidate Milton Shapp in his unsuccessful 1966 gubernatorial bid. At the time there was some speculation that the paper's opposition was based on Shapp's interest in Jerrold Electronics, a firm in competition with Triangle's cable television operations. Shapp had also been instrumental in blocking Triangle's grab for the exclusive rights for cable television in Philadelphia. A political friend of Annenberg's had attempted to slip the enabling legislation through the City Council by burying it in an innocuous street-improvement bill, but Shapp found out about it and led opposition that resulted in Triangle's having to split the city up with five other firms.

Walter Annenberg himself, however, almost readily acknowledges what he considers the primary reason for the *Inquirer*'s opposition to Shapp, the fact that the candidate made his objection to the merger of the Pennsylvania and New York Central railroads one of the principal campaign issues.

"I had a sympathetic view toward Mr. Shapp long before the campaign," explains Annenberg, "but then he used the Pennsylvania Railroad as his *schtick*. Do you know what a *schtick* is? It's a show-business term, a device used to draw attention to yourself. The Pennsylvania

Railroad was Mr. Shapp's *schtick,* a publicity gimmick he used for political purposes. I've always been tremendously interested in the Pennsylvania Railroad; it is one of the great American corporations and has played an important role in the history and growth of our country and this community. Stuart Saunders, the chairman of the board and chief executive officer, is a personal friend of mine and we've had a warm and stimulating relationship serving the Pennsylvania."

In explaining the rationale behind the *Inquirer*'s opposition to Shapp, Annenberg implicitly acknowledges one of the most vicious editorial campaigns ever conducted against any political candidate by any newspaper. It featured, in addition to legitimate comment on its editorial page, consistently slanted news stories, and blatant distortion of the facts.

Milton Shapp was painted as an irresponsible, intemperate quack lustily craving for the governor's seat in order to initiate policies that would bankrupt the state. "It was pure character assassination," noted a political observer at the time, "and if a Pulitzer Prize were given for yellow journalism, the *Inquirer* would have it wrapped up." A nationally syndicated columnist, up from Washington a few days during the campaign, said he had never seen anything like it in his thirty years of reporting. So excessive did the *Inquirer*'s unfair coverage become that even Shapp's rival, Governor Raymond Shafer, confided to a friend that he was beginning to worry that the backlash might hurt him.

And, just as Annenberg admits, the start of it can be

traced back to the specific day that Shapp said the railroad merger "was a legalized multimillion-dollar swindle
which put the robber barons of old to shame." The next
day the top editorial in the *Inquirer* was titled: "Rabble-
Rousing Irresponsibility." It characterized Shapp's statement as "disgusting" and said he had "overstepped all
bounds of decency and honesty in seeking to picture the
officials involved in the railroad merger as 'robber barons'
engaged in a huge 'swindle.' "

Readers of the *Inquirer* soon began getting the impression that Shapp had called respected Pennsy chairman Stuart Saunders a robber baron. In fact, the writer
of the paper's Sunday news roundup said that specifically,
but he wasn't the only one misled by the *Inquirer*'s coverage. At the height of the paper's vitriolic attacks a mutual friend of Shapp and Annenberg attempted to smooth
things over by calling the publisher. Mrs. Annenberg
answered the telephone and when the friend explained
why he wanted to talk with her husband she blurted:
"Why, that man called Stuart Saunders a robber baron!"

The *Inquirer*'s techniques in knifing Shapp were
totally without finesse. Where an editorial stiletto would
have sufficed, it used a blunt hatchet. At one point a cur-
sory reader of the paper would come away with the con-
fused impression that Shapp had paid off every Negro
minister in Pennsylvania in order to win the primary
and, at the same time, bought his mailing list from a
white supremacist. When a man who once worked for
Shapp as an errand boy at seventy-five dollars a week was
arrested on a completely nonpolitical criminal charge,

the *Inquirer* blasted the story across its first page with the screaming headline: SHAPP EX-AIDE ARRESTED. It also promoted the man to a "public relations specialist" and raised his salary to $125 a week.

The newspaper, naturally, salivated tremendously when a group of "taxpayers," led by Philadelphia Republican City Committee counsel Edward Becker, filed a petition in Dauphin County Court asking for an audit of Shapp's primary-campaign expenses. A gusher of distorted headlines and slanted news stories sprang from its pages. However, the last day of the hearing provides an excellent comparative example of the *Inquirer*'s coverage.

Here are some samples of how some other papers around the state headlined the story—Allentown *Morning Call:* JUDGE HITS CHALLENGE OF SHAPP EXPENSES, DEMANDS WITNESSES. Johnstown *Tribune Democrat:* ANTI-SHAPP GROUP HIT BY JUDGE. Harrisburg *Patriot:* COURT WARNS GOP TO SHOW EVIDENCE IN SHAPP AUDIT CASE. Easton *Express:* JUDGE REBUKES LAWYER FOR GOP IN SHAPP CASE. Pittsburgh *Press:* RECEIPTS UNSTUDIED, SHAPP FOES ADMIT. Philadelphia *Bulletin:* JUDGE RAPS ACCUSERS IN SHAPP EXPENSE AUDIT. These headlines reflected the crux of the story, which was that Dauphin County Judge Homer Kreider said that it seemed the petitioners had "trifled with this court and the taxpayers" and that they "haven't called a single witness" to support their allegations.

On this *same* story the *Inquirer*'s headline was: KEY WITNESS EVADES QUIZ AS AUDIT OF MAIN SHAPP ACCOUNT

ENDS. Its lead pointed out that Harvey F. Johnston, founder and president of the National Association for the Advancement of White People, never testified at the hearing. Nowhere in the story did it mention what, if any, relationship Johnston had with Shapp. But it pointed out in a very conspiratorial tone: "The founder of the racist organization himself had been a candidate for the Democratic nomination, but withdrew in favor of Shapp."

The undercover techniques the *Inquirer* used in attempting to dig for dirt on Shapp were as reprehensible as its news coverage. Old associates and friends were called and asked leading questions about his "mental health" and his "other problems." Ace staffer Harry Karafin went around town bragging he was going to "smear" Shapp by finding out why he changed his name from Shapiro. After threatening legal action when he heard rumors spreading that the paper had information about him being in a mental hospital, Shapp received a call from political reporter Joe Miller. "Is it true you said you'd sue if we ran a story about you being in an institution?" Miller asked. "Yes," said Shapp. "Then you deny it?" asked Miller. Shapp said he did. The next day the *Inquirer* ran a short piece saying that Shapp denied he was ever in a mental institution.

The bulk of the digging and reporting on the Shapp campaign was directly assigned to Harry Karafin and Joe Miller, at that time two of the paper's most experienced specialists. Others, however, were pressed into the hatchet job when needed, among them Saul Kohler,

since promoted to chief of the *Inquirer*'s Washington
bureau. Kohler later confided to a friend the effect of
such assignments. "My hands drip blood for days," he
said.

What, in retrospect, makes the *Inquirer*'s bitter attack
on Shapp significant in relation to any assessment of
Walter Annenberg's character is that at the time it was
not public knowledge that Annenberg was the largest
individual stockholder of the Pennsylvania Railroad.

It was revealed only after the gubernatorial campaign
was over, and then as a result of Annenberg's election to
the company's board of directors.

What raises an additional and perhaps more relevant
question is the fact that, aside from the Shapp campaign,
*Inquirer* editorials had consistently urged consummation
of the merger in the "public interest."

In fact, *Inquirer* editorials often pressed for the merger
so strongly—without ever revealing Annenberg's financial interest in it—that it frequently distorted a basic
sense of perspective. When the United States Supreme
Court, for instance, voted to delay the merger until the
Interstate Commerce Commission could further study its
possible economic consequences for smaller railroads, an
*Inquirer* editorial praised Justice Abe Fortas's negative
vote as one of the great dissenting opinions of all time,
among those that have been "outstanding in their discerning probe for the truth." Justice Fortas (who later
resigned from the Supreme Court with his own conflict-
of-interest problems) had written: "The court's decision

in this case is wrong in principle and unfortunate in consequence."

How could readers of Annenberg's newspaper not assume, in learning of his financial holdings in the railroad, an inherent conflict between these two interests?

That was the question Walter Annenberg himself was recently asked. "What do I care what they think," he said matter-of-factly, "as long as I know in my own mind that they're completely different?"

Annenberg obviously and apparently sincerely believed he had enough strength of character not to permit his financial interests to interfere with his editorial judgment. (Many years ago a young publisher less sure of his ability to withstand temptation turned down a trusted friend's offer of $150,000 worth of municipal advertising with no strings attached because he was afraid the windfall, though badly needed at the time, might cause him to adjust his editorial posture; his name was Adolph Ochs and his paper was *The New York Times*.)

There may be a possibility, of course, that in acquiring his huge bloc of shares in the Pennsylvania Railroad, Annenberg was not interested primarily in its profit potential. What he may have had most in mind was the honor of sitting alongside some of the most socially prestigious businessmen in the country on its board of directors. Long snubbed by class society and forever struggling to emerge from the shadow of his father's public ignominy, it meant a good deal for Walter Annenberg to rub elbows with such socially prominent figures

as Pittsburgh financier Richard K. Mellon and investment banker Howard Butcher III. (An ironic note, by
the way, is that Butcher eventually decided to resign
from the board of the merged Penn Central because of
a "potential conflict of interest" of his own. Company
chairman Stuart Saunders praised his decision as "an act
of business statesmanship.")

Whatever Annenberg's motives in acquiring his interest in the Pennsylvania Railroad, the fact is that he used
the news and editorial forces of his newspaper to enhance
that interest. And there are other instances of assignments he has caused to be undertaken that reflect his
willingness to use his press powers.

o o o

One of those assignments Joe Goulden remembers
vividly. Goulden, a tall, hefty, no-nonsense Texan, was
recruited by the *Inquirer* when it was desperately trying
to rebuild its staff following a long and bitter strike by
the Newspaper Guild in 1959. It was then that Annenberg had made an administrative blunder that was to
affect the quality of the paper for years to come. Angry
and disillusioned at what he considered the ingratitude
of his employees for walking out on strike, Annenberg
offered in his settlement to give severance pay to any
reporter who wanted to quit. This, he hoped, would get
rid of the ringleaders of the strike. It did. It also got rid
of the best men on the paper, those who could easily get
jobs elsewhere while also pocketing as much as a year's
salary. Mostly it was the veterans who remained, the older

deskmen entrenched in their sinecures. What followed were trying times for the *Inquirer*. Goulden recalls his shock as a newcomer in learning that a big-city daily often had only three reporters on the street, one of them hastily promoted from copy boy. Sometimes the first edition of the paper would consist entirely of wire-service stories and pieces rewritten from earlier *Bulletin* clippings.

Eventually, however, the staff was rebuilt to a somewhat respectable size and Goulden quickly hustled his way up to become one of the *Inquirer*'s best and most respected reporters. His reputation was such that when the time came he was given the assignment of writing the paper's own denunciation of Harry Karafin. It was an assignment that Goulden handled with vengeance and anger because he himself felt personally betrayed by what he considered the most odious of humans, a newspaperman gone wrong.

Like most men who daily bend rigid ideals to meet their own and their family's self-interest, Goulden was no fundamental moralist, but he somehow felt his integrity threatened when, a few years ago, E. Z. Dimitman told him that Annenberg wanted an article about a businessman named Matthew Fox, one that would "knock the hell out of him."

Goulden couldn't figure out why Annenberg wanted an article about Fox, who wasn't a Philadelphian and had no interests in the area. And he wasn't told; he was ordered simply to go to Washington and collect the needed information from an Annenberg contact on the

Federal Communications Commission. In Washington, Goulden found that Fox's career would make a hatchet job simple. A former vice-president of Universal Pictures and husband of Yolande Betbeze, Miss America of 1951, Fox was not a guy in a white hat. A wheeler-dealer who had once been in trouble with the SEC, he was credited with financing the coup that brought Indonesia strong-man Sukarno to power, a deal in which Fox was to get all of that country's mineral, oil, export, and import rights.

Goulden also discovered, however, what might have been the key to Annenberg's interest in Fox. At the time Fox was in a deal with Lear-Siegler, a Santa Monica elec-tronics firm, in backing something called Subscription Television Inc. This was a $30-million corporation attempting the first major effort to get pay television off the ground. A raging battle against it was being fought in Southern California, its experimental territory. A million-dollar war fund was being raised to fight it by its two major enemies, the movie exhibitors and the pro-ducers of free television shows. Many thought the suc-cess of pay TV could destroy free TV by putting the control of the box office in the hands of the viewers in-stead of sponsors. Such control would mean that pay TV could easily outbid free TV for talent, material, and production facilities and thus wind up with the fattest slice of daily television programming. And that, in turn, would mean that an outfit like Fox's could produce its own listings for its television programs and knock the pins out from under a publication like *TV Guide,* then fast becoming the most lucrative Triangle operation.

Goulden stewed over his assignment for nineteen days. He had checked into the Willard Hotel, each morning ordered a bottle of Jack Daniel's, and each day drowned his dilemma in it. ("My expense account became an *Inquirer* legend," he recalls.) Finally, when he was ordered to return to Philadelphia with a finished article, Goulden produced the most vicious, derogatory piece he could about Fox. As he had hoped, it was checked with the *Inquirer*'s lawyers, judged much too libelous, and never printed.

∘ ∘ ∘

Another instance in which Walter Annenberg's editorial motives seemed to have some connection with his financial interests was the series of articles he ordered attacking Philadelphia businessman Herbert J. Siegel's attempts to gain control of Paramount Pictures Corporation. Although Siegel's name had previously gotten into the *Inquirer* only in small squibs buried at the bottom of its business news pages, Annenberg ordered full, front-page coverage of a court battle in New York challenging Siegel's efforts to take over Paramount. While *Inquirer* reporters are not usually sent out of town, a man was assigned especially to New York to handle the stories, which were consistently slanted and prejudicially headlined. What a Philadelphia newspaper said about a New York court case would not normally have a prejudicial impact on that case, but at the time the newspapers were on strike in New York and the *Inquirer* was selling more than 100,000 copies there daily. And its stories were indeed rigged. Siegel was repeatedly described as a corporate "raider" and pictured as a power-hungry vulture who used stockholders' money from one firm to buy himself control of another.

What the *Inquirer* stories didn't point out, however, was that one of Paramount's fattest assets was its stock of old movies. Although Paramount had earlier sold its string of four hundred theatres to the American Broadcasting Corporation, it had refused to sell the actual movies. ABC didn't appreciate that, nor the fact that if Siegel acquired Paramount another television network would pay a high price for those movies. The *Inquirer* stories also neglected to point out that leading the fight against Siegel were friends of Annenberg's with an interest in ABC and that one of those friends was supplying the *Inquirer* reporter with all the "inside" information on the case. Annenberg's WFIL stations in Philadelphia are affiliated with the ABC network.

∘ ∘ ∘

In view of Annenberg's own assurance that he kept such conflicts of interest "completely different" in his own mind, the question is on what justification did he base such infringement on the *Inquirer*'s editorial responsibility? The answer must rest on the assumption that those who engaged his wrath he considered worthy of legitimate criticism. They are men whose own interests he judged ill-motivated. The fact that the *Inquirer's* news columns had to be manipulated in order to expose such individuals to the public was, he must believe, merely the means to achieve an honorable end.

That was known, among some of his own employees, as Annenberg's "Big Daddy" syndrome.

"I've always said that we common folk have to thank God for Walter Annenberg and the *Inquirer*," claims a local public relations man, tongue in cheek. "If it weren't for that newspaper we wouldn't know when to fly our flags! That's what really gripes me about the *Inquirer*. Everything from a Dell concert to a Thrill Show to flying the flag from our homes is taken over and enveloped in its Great Father approach. Orwell never wrote it so well."

One of the most revealing manifestations of Annenberg's "Big Daddy" attitude occurred only a few days after the dedication of the Annenberg School of Communications at Penn, where president Gaylord Harnwell (who had not yet been blacklisted) extolled the publisher as "a public-spirited citizen, deeply committed to freedom of communications." If Harnwell had prescience, he would have choked on his words, because within the week Philadelphia was rocking with a blatant display of Walter Annenberg's power of censorship.

It involved an American Broadcasting Company television program produced by veteran newscaster Howard K. Smith and keyed to Richard Nixon's defeat the previous week in the California gubernatorial election and his subsequent announcement that he was retiring from politics. The half-hour show, entitled *The Political Obituary of Richard Nixon,* was produced as part of a regular Sunday-evening public affairs series, but because of its timeliness was scheduled to pre-empt a Veteran's Day documentary, *The American Fighting Man.*

The Saturday before the show was scheduled, the Associated Press carried a story about the program change and reported that the Nixon documentary would include filmed interviews with four people who had figured prominently in his career: one was his campaign manager, another a close Congressional associate, a third the man he had defeated in his first bid for public office, and the fourth Alger Hiss, a former State Department official who was convicted of perjury in 1950 when he denied he delivered certain documents to a Communist spy ring. Nixon, then a member of the House Un-American Activities Committee, helped break the case. The disclosures jetted Nixon from relative obscurity into national prominence and thence to the Senate and the vice-presidency.

Walter Annenberg watched that Associated Press story come across the ticker in his Wynnewood home that Saturday afternoon. (The wire-service machine is in a closet in his library and during the week his wife would turn it on for him just prior to his arriving home.) On Sunday morning the *Inquirer* carried a small box on its front page headlined: TV SHOW IS "KILLED."

The box announced that Walter Annenberg had instructed his two ABC-affiliated stations—WFIL-TV in Philadelphia and WNHC-TV in New Haven—not to carry the Smith program. It quoted the stations' owner as saying: "I cannot see that any useful purpose would be served in permitting a convicted treasonable spy [sic] to comment about a distinguished American." (A deskman had pointed out the mistake but managing editor John Gillen told him: "Let it run the way the publisher dictated it.")

No mention was made of the fact that the Hiss appearance was part of an attempt at a balanced format, that other individuals would provide a favorable view of Nixon, or that the head of ABC's public-affairs section, the man responsible for approving the programming, was James Hagerty, presidential press secretary during the Eisenhower-Nixon administration.

All day Sunday the switchboard at WFIL-TV was flooded with irate telephone calls. Over 1,500 reached the station before the show was scheduled at 10:30. At the appointed time the station cut out the network pick-up and screened a half-hour documentary on Telstar dug out of its videotape files. Another 600 calls rapidly poured in from viewers who had expected to see the Nixon show.

Although controversial reaction to television shows often makes news in itself, Monday's *Inquirer* had everything coming up roses. It ran a front-page headline: VETERANS GROUPS HAIL DECISION NOT TO AIR HISS TV APPEARANCE. "Veterans organization leaders lauded the *Inquirer* Sunday night for its stand against the appearance of Alger Hiss on an ABC-TV network program," said the story.

There was no indication that the television show had

become a national *cause célèbre* as a result of reaction
from Nixon supporters across the country who were
claiming that the inclusion of the Hiss interview was
an exercise in bad judgment by the network. Annenberg
would have undoubtedly preferred to print that information, but since Philadelphia viewers did not—by his
decree—have the opportunity to see the show, it would
only have aroused their interest in something they knew
nothing about. Thus the *Inquirer* suppressed a thirty-
three-inch Associated Press story detailing the national
furor.

Annenberg's television station had a more difficult
time keeping the story from reaching its audience. At
that time WFIL-TV was picking up two network news
shows from ABC, one at 7 P.M. and the other at 11. Since
the earlier show was videotaped, it was easy enough to
scissor the reference to the Nixon show. On the live 11
o'clock show, however, nervous local monitors blacked
out the network commentator in mid-sentence.

Annenberg's censorship directive made it even tougher
for WFIL radio. Since the station hooked into the network for five minutes of national news every hour, an
advance call to New York had to be made prior to the
hour all day long in order to ascertain the exact minute
and second the Nixon item would be mentioned. Once
that was done, a bit of local news of exactly the same air
length had to be written so that it could be beeped in as
a replacement. A few times during the day, the trickiness
of the operation resulted in dead air.

The affair, however, wouldn't die and it became obvious to Annenberg that it would become more and more difficult to keep it buried. Then, three days after the show, the *Inquirer* finally alluded to the fracas it was causing around the nation. In a page-three "Letter From the Editor" box, Annenberg acknowledged "the thoughtfulness and interest of those who wrote, telephoned and telegraphed," and amplified on why he ordered the program killed. "It seemed to me," he wrote, "that the use of a spy, convicted of perjury [his lawyers had presumably advised him of the correct nature of the charge], to sit in judgment on a distinguished American who loyally served his country in war and in high public office, would be repugnant to most viewers." He then claimed that his action was not politically motivated and, in substantiation, pointed out that the *Inquirer* had just recently censured Nixon for his attacks on the press following his California defeat. "It is my belief," Annenberg concluded, "that these decisions of news evaluation were valid and in the public interest."

Annenberg might have really believed that, but his statement itself raised a serious question about his true concern for the public interest, because in it he again neglected to mention that Hiss's appearance took only two minutes of what was a balanced thirty-minute show; that he had actually censored news programs on both his television and radio stations; and that the *Inquirer* was continuing to suppress wire-service stories about the controversy the show had aroused across the nation.

Nor would it be irrational to raise doubts about Annenberg's political disclaimer, considering his staunch support of Nixon down through the years and Nixon's recent recognition of that support by naming him ambassador to England. As far back as the 1952 election, when the revelation of a special fund for the vice-presidential candidate rocked the nation and newspapers across the country bannered the news, the *Inquirer* looked the other way, kept the story off the front page until the second day, then announced: NIXON'S EXPLANATION OF FUND ACCEPTED BY EISENHOWER; TO GET ACCOUNTING.

When that story broke, by the way, the *Inquirer* had a columnist named Frank Brookhouser who happened to be on vacation. When he returned he wrote an innocuous column of casual observations, one-sentence comments on a variety of subjects. One of them: "The people I know were not too impressed by Nixon's 'Checkers' speech." (Nixon's dog, Checkers, had appeared with him on his nationwide television explanation of the fund.) That brief crack at Nixon caused what Brookhouser recalls as "a bombshell reaction." His column was reduced, shoved deeper into the paper, and, later, his byline was removed. Brookhouser quit and went to the *Bulletin*.

(The Nixons subsequently have become even closer to the Annenbergs. As Vice President, Nixon frequently was a guest of the publisher at his Wynnewood estate, and when he returned from his 1958 trip to South America during which he was stoned by angry mobs his first stop was with the Annenbergs in Philadelphia. After he left the vice-presidency, the *Inquirer* was the paper

that broke the story of his joining a New York law firm.
That story, by the way, contained no comment or analy-
sis if what it meant for a former Vice President to abandon his political base in California, nor was any source
for the facts mentioned.)

There have been numerous other instances where
Annenberg's political partisanship has been directly
manifested in the *Inquirer's* operations. Harold Stassen
made the blacklist by attempting to knock Nixon out
of his second nomination for the vice-presidency. When
the late conservative congressman Francis E. Walter,
chairman of the House Un-American Activities Committee (long one of Annenberg's very favorite groups),
was in political trouble in his Eastern Pennsylvania district, Annenberg ordered an eight-part series ghost-
written under Walter's byline. The series detailed the
Communist menace and Walter's fight against it, and
after it ran in the *Inquirer* Annenberg had it reprinted
in booklet form and distributed in Walter's district.

Whether it be outright censorship, slanted coverage,
or biased presentation of a story, Annenberg gave more
consideration to his own motivations than he did to the
journalistic principle of a sacrosanct news operation. If
Annenberg deliberately violated the paper's editorial integrity, it was undoubtedly because he believed he had
the right as its publisher to do so. In fact, he probably
believed that's the way all publications should be run.

A number of years ago, for instance, *Time* magazine,
the national news weekly, ran a piece in its "Press" section about the *Inquirer's* coverage of the murder of

Henry Turner, an *Inquirer* truck driver beaten to death in its parking lot. While the *Daily News,* at that time still in Matt McCloskey's hands, was blasting out news of the case as a running story, *Time* pointed out that the *Inquirer* had quickly dropped any mention of it. *Time* also quoted district attorney Victor Blanc as charging that the motive in Turner's murder "involves payroll padding and padding of overtime pay on the *Inquirer.*"

In response to *Time*'s piece, Annenberg had *Inquirer* managing editor John Gillen write a letter of objection for publication in *Time*'s "Letters to the Editor" section. Gillen accused the magazine of "bad reporting." Annenberg then sent Gillen's letter, plus a covering note from himself, to *Time* president James Linen (who happens to be former governor William Scranton's brother-in-law). Annenberg said he would like Gillen's letter to be "used at an early date," and implied that he wouldn't be unhappy if Linen saw fit to fire *Time*'s Philadelphia correspondent, who was a *Bulletin* reporter. ("All of us at the *Inquirer,*" wrote Annenberg, "still feel very strongly about the lack of objectivity.")

Linen refused to play ball. *Time*'s correspondent, he said, was doing "a competent and responsible job" and Gillen's objections were both factually inaccurate and irrelevant. He also answered Gillen directly: "Walter Annenberg asked that we publish your comments but . . . I'm sure you will understand why we feel we would not be justified in doing so."

The Turner case, which, by the way, was never officially closed, also had other interesting aspects. Annenberg never forgave district attorney Blanc for making public the charges about payroll padding and loan-shark activities at the *Inquirer*. And Blanc very shortly found out the power of Annenberg's wrath. Not long after the Turner case was hot news, Blanc picked up the *Inquirer* one morning and read that Mayor Richardson Dilworth would oppose his renomination for office and that, furthermore, "the Mayor hates Victor Blanc and the district attorney's feelings are mutual."

Dilworth today claims that he never discussed his opposition to Blanc with Annenberg and, as a matter of fact, objected to Blanc's renomination because of his failure to be a "vigorous and effective district attorney." But Blanc, on the other hand, has said that he felt the *Inquirer* story was a mistake and that as soon as it appeared he called Dilworth and said, "Dick, there's a terrible story in today's *Inquirer* that you know is a lie." According to Blanc, Dilworth's answer was silence. He wouldn't deny the story. Although he had his eye on the governor's seat at the time and his law firm was pocketing a fat retainer as the *Inquirer*'s legal counsel, Dilworth today denies such facts were relevant to his refusal to back Blanc.

There was a prior instance, however, when Dilworth—normally never a man to duck a fight—definitely exhibited a reluctance to tangle with the Annenberg might. It was about the time that Philadelphia's much-heralded renewal program, the nation's pioneering urban-reformation project, was just getting off the ground. The Citizens Committee on City Planning, a group of nonpartisan civic leaders, inaugurated a drive to widen the major thoroughfare of Vine Street, a traffic-clogged artery that cut across the center of the city and had to be dealt with before other major projects could be undertaken. The Citizens Committee asked Dilworth to become chairman of the drive to arouse public support for the important project. What made the task a ticklish one was that the widening of Vine Street meant destroying many homes which, although in slum areas, were part of solidly controlled voting blocs and the political strongholds of some influential city bosses. One politician with strength in the area was old Municipal Court judge Charles A. Brown, a very close friend of Walter Annenberg. Brown soon convinced Annenberg to oppose the Vine Street widening. When Dilworth heard of Annenberg's opposition, he immediately stepped down from the chairmanship of the Citizens Committee drive. The tough former U.S. Marine wasn't quite ready to face up to the powerful publisher. He did, after all, want to be mayor of Philadelphia one day.

o o o

The Philadelphia *Inquirer* is a major metropolitan newspaper, a business organization that employs more than 3,000 persons, including 250 men and women whose job it is to produce the guts of the product, its editorial content. Yet it is doubtful that even *one* of those individuals would contend that the *Inquirer* represented in tone or spirit or outlook an amalgamation of the fullest talents of the professionals who produced it.

The Philadelphia *Inquirer* represented Walter Annenberg, no more and no less. And because he was so determined that the paper play an important role in the community, it embarked on many an editorial campaign that had a very positive effect on Philadelphia. From its successful crusade against the use of firecrackers to its important role in getting the corrupt magistrate system revamped, the *Inquirer* compiled an impressive record of public service. And almost every initiating idea came from Annenberg himself. It was he who set the paper's aspirations as well as imposed its limitations. He may not, even as its "editor," have been aware of every word in it every day, but there was not an edition printed that was not carefully tailored to his thinking, his attitudes, his political philosophy, his interests, his character, his very essence. To accomplish this delicate task took a group of loyal associates, alert to his volatile temperament and whims, responsive to every nuance of his desires.

For almost the entire period of Walter Annenberg's control of the *Inquirer,* E. Z. Dimitman was his top editorial lieutenant. (He was the only editorial employee who had an office, prickled with an impressive collection of potted cacti, on the twelfth floor with Annenberg's.) A thin, round-shouldered man with a sandy gray mustache and thick-lensed glasses, Dimitman often looked like a tallish Groucho Marx, head thrust forward, hands deep in his pockets, big cigar and loud sport jacket, stalking through the city room to whisper "special assignments," direct from the twelfth floor, to a select few. "The publisher's chewing the carpet again," Dimitman was heard to say in announcing such assignments.

Dimitman is Annenberg's idea of a newspaperman, a former city editor out of the *Front Page* school, Chicago style. As a matter of fact, he was the city editor of the *Inquirer* when Moe Annenberg bought the paper, having joined it as a rewriteman in 1925. Before he went to jail, Moe had promoted him to executive editor over the heads of some older veterans. Dimitman had caught Moe's eye when he accepted responsibility for the bootlegged publication of an important State Supreme Court decision before it was officially handed down, and though Moe denied knowledge of it on the witness stand, he considered it a smart piece of strategy.

Dimitman left the *Inquirer* shortly after Walter Annenberg took over and worked for a few years on papers in Chicago and Newark. He reportedly rubbed the young Annenberg the wrong way by continuing to treat him with the same lack of deference he had before the old man died. When he returned to the *Inquirer* he became the one man most responsible for helping to shape the newspaper to the character of its publisher. Called recently and asked to discuss that role, he graciously declined for what he said were "a good many reasons."

Dimitman is a nuts-and-bolts newspaperman who knows about such things as printing fonts and good make-up and jazzy headlines. He reportedly did such a great job in brightening up the paper when Moe Annenberg took over, the appreciative Moe presented him

with a $1,000 platinum Swiss watch so fancy and be-
gadgeted that office wags claimed a little man popped
out of it on the hour to announce race results at Hialeah.

Another key individual in the *Inquirer*'s news operation was managing editor John Gillen. According to one
staffer, Gillen was made managing editor several years
ago because "he looks like a managing editor." Dimitman
was the one who reportedly backed him for the slot, and,
like him, Gillen has the talent of blocking out a snappy
front-page layout with a few flicks of a grease pencil.
"I think Dimmy picked Gillen because he knew he would
be loyal and not graspingly ambitious, not the type of
guy who would undermine him," says a former top
editor.

A personable, handsome, wavy-haired Irish Catholic
(the *Inquirer* itself pointed out his religion in announcing his promotion), Gillen was not considered by the
paper's staff to be an old-style, hard-nosed managing
editor. Although up from the staff Gillen showed he
was not journalistically constricted in his thinking. It was
he who was largely responsible for attempting to broaden
the paper's style, appeal, and readability by instituting
the "Passing Scene" column. For a while, *Inquirer* readers gasped at the obvious freedom of expression and
choice of topics that columnists Joe McGinniss and Rose
DeWolf were enjoying, but eventually Annenberg himself tightened the wrench and both resigned in disgust,
McGinniss to write a best-selling book about how Madi-
son Avenue advertising techniques helped win Richard
Nixon the presidential election.

Although Gillen had been known to let an Annenberg-proscribed item slip into print occasionally, he generally adhered to a don't-rock-the-boat philosophy. He occasionally voiced disagreement with Annenberg, but there is no evidence that Gillen ever took a firm stand against any of the publisher's journalistic excesses. For example, when his favorite State Supreme Court Justice died not long ago, Annenberg told Gillen that he wanted it noted in Musmanno's obituary that one of the probable causes of the man's death was the "terrible maligning" he had taken from his long-time political opponent Senator Joseph Clark. Gillen said that sort of thing really had no place in a news story and that if Annenberg wanted it mentioned he should put it in an editorial page comment. Annenberg, however, was adamant and insisted it be part of the obit. Gillen simply stewed and fretted, feeling that there was nothing he could do. Annenberg, however, called him about a half hour after he issued the directive and said, "You're right, John. That shouldn't be in an obituary."

While the managing editor of a newspaper is normally the field commander of its editorial forces, Gillen always kept himself rather aloof from the *Inquirer*'s news staff. His office did not adjoin the city room and he was only an occasional visitor to it. (Compared to Annenberg, however, Gillen was practically omnipresent. There are some staffers on the *Inquirer* who had never even seen the editor of the paper, and most never personally met him. One key deskman, a quarter-century veteran, did only once.) For most of the last three decades, the man who was responsible for the daily collection of the *Inquirer*'s editorial content was stubby, balding, weary-faced executive city editor Morrie Litman, who just recently "retired."

Everyone liked Morrie Litman. Not everyone trusted his journalistic motives or agreed with his professional approach, but everyone thought he was a great guy. Loyal to the tenets of old-style, get-the-story-at-all-costs newspapering, Litman was, in fact, brought to the *Inquirer* from the *Ledger* by his mentor, E. Z. Dimitman. It was Litman who was the on-the-line enforcer of Annenberg's explicit and implicit directives and who on occasion could be seen dictating the first few paragraphs of a story to a rewriteman who couldn't quite achieve the desired approach.

Litman's primary interest was in local politics and his contacts and close associations with the boys in the political backrooms were extensive. His two primary sources of "inside" information, however, were Police Captain Clarence Ferguson, head of the Special Investigations Squad, and Harry Karafin.

For many years, Ferguson—perhaps in atonement for his role in Moe Annenberg's troubles (he reported an attempted bribe) or perhaps in exchange for a lack of close *Inquirer* scrutiny of his own methods of operation—has been an unofficial reporter for Annenberg's newspaper. He would often dictate the news of his own drug or gambling raids directly to a rewriteman. It has become something of a standing routine that he is always asked, "Is this the biggest haul you ever made, Captain?"

and his inevitable answer is, "Oh yeah, this is the biggest." Ferguson's raids have always gotten special handling at the *Inquirer,* and that is not unrelated to the fact that he, Litman, and often John Gillen met regularly for dinner together at least once a week.

As for convicted blackmailer Harry Karafin, Morrie Litman has said that he was "my eyes and my ears." When his desk assignment kept him from moving through the slippery alleys of the city's world of wheelers and dealers, it was Karafin who went out and did his sniffing for him and brought him back the behind-the-scenes reports. "I would have trusted him with my life," Litman testified at Karafin's trial. "No one can forget—or discredit—Morrie's testimony," a colleague later wrote in tribute. "A naïve and possibly absurd confession, but certainly in keeping with the kind of humanism Morrie practiced and made his article of faith."

Soon after the Karafin trial ended, orders came down from the top that executive city editor Litman was to be released, permitted to step into "retirement." To go with him was city editor Phil Schaeffer. Litman docilely withdrew; Schaeffer, resenting the implication, refused and was fired. Gillen, in arguing against the dismissal, reportedly told Annenberg that Schaeffer had absolutely no relationship with Karafin. Annenberg's reply: "I didn't say that he did."

Schaeffer was something of an anomaly at the *Inquirer,* a man completely without cunning or guile, as honest as the Sunday school teacher that he was. His lack of tough surface mannerisms led many of the more hardened veteran reporters to refer to him, behind his back, of course, as "Philsy." Schaeffer was an ex-Marine who didn't act like one, a man who managed to remain so naïvely aloof from the bitter turmoil of city room politics that one staffer once remarked in amazement: "Schaeffer's the only guy in this rumble without a shiv."

Schaeffer had been with the *Inquirer* for less than six years, having spent most of his career with the *Bulletin*. The transition, he later told a friend, was unsettling. "I had worked for a paper where the only time I ever remember the owner interfering with news operations was when someone wrote something about a rider being thrown from his horse," Schaeffer said. "A memo was sent to the newsroom explaining that a horse *never* throws a rider; a rider falls from a horse because he doesn't know how to ride."

When Schaeffer went to the *Inquirer* he stepped into city editor Morrie Litman's slot, with Litman given the title of executive city editor. Old-timers looked for fireworks, but Schaeffer and Litman got along well. In fact, at times it seemed as if they weren't even working for the same newspaper. The tight clique of veteran reporters who had been loyal to city editor Litman continued to report to executive city editor Litman; the younger men, and those Schaeffer himself hired later, reported to the new city editor.

While Schaeffer was considered something of a liberal by *Inquirer* standards ("Any good cause could get a story from him," recalls a staffer), many on the paper didn't respect his news judgment or his timorous approach to explosive stories. Like Gillen, he also wasn't the type of guy who would deliberately rock the boat.

But then again, who could? Annenberg's strong control and pervasive hand in the *Inquirer*'s news operation injected a kind of schizophrenia into the very aura of the city room. While frantically attempting to immerse themselves in the coverage of the day's fast-breaking news, the paper's editors also had to maintain a constant awareness of the publisher's own interests and concerns. According to a former editor, "Everything was always handled with one question in mind: How would Annenberg want this played?"

*How would Annenberg want this played?* Such a consideration has to have a horrendous effect on any objective approach to handling and presenting the news. There were, of course, numerous occasions when, at the very least, it upset normal city room activity. Managing editor Gillen, for instance, more than once received a call from the "editor" asking if ample coverage was going to be given to the dedication of, say, a new wing to some West Philadelphia hospital in which he or one of his friends might have a social or charitable interest. Gillen would quickly assure his boss that the story was going to get prominent play. Yes sir, photo and all. Then he would frantically dash out and send half the available staff scurrying off to cover the event, which he had previously decided wasn't worth an inch of valuable news space.

Annenberg's interests, however, often got consideration without any specific orders from him that they should. Joe Goulden recalls that following the *Inquirer*'s public vomiting of Karafin, it was decided to go after all those individuals and organizations that were involved in his affairs. As part of that effort, Goulden dug up a good deal of information about certain notes held by the First Pennsylvania Bank, one of Karafin's "clients." These were mostly consumer installment loans generated by fast-buck operators, home-repair dealers, rug salesmen, and the like, and acquired by the bank from third parties. Goulden had gone as far as California for some of his information. When he came back with the story, Gillen told him to forget it. "We can't run a story like that," Gillen said. "Annenberg's own bank has the same stuff." (Annenberg was then a member of the board of Girard Trust.)

Joe Goulden claims, by the way, that in his more than seven years with the paper he saw little evidence of Annenberg's concern for comprehensive, consistent, and accurate coverage of major news stories. He points, as an example, to a time when an *Inquirer* editor went so far as to rewrite history, apparently without upsetting Annenberg's sense of journalistic ethics.

Goulden was in the Washington bureau at the time, covering the Senate Foreign Relations Committee hearings on the Tonkin incidents. These concerned attacks on two United States destroyers by North Vietnam in the Gulf of Tonkin. President Johnson used the attacks, allegedly unprovoked and unexpected, as a basis for instituting retaliatory bombings of North Vietnam. During the hearings, Goulden, who was conversant enough with the issues involved to later write a book on the Tonkin incidents, filed a story saying that testimony revealed that the captain of one of the destroyers had told superiors two days *before* the attack that he was in a dangerous position off the North Vietnam coast, feared that he would be attacked, and asked permission to break off the mission.

That, in effect, was also the gist of the story as carried the next day in such respected newspapers as *The New York Times*, the Washington *Post*, the Baltimore *Sun*, and, in fact, by the wire services.

However, when an *Inquirer* veteran assistant managing editor—a man credited with thinking more like Annenberg than Annenberg himself—received Goulden's copy from Washington, he took it upon himself to rewrite the lead:

> WASHINGTON, Feb. 24—The United States did not provoke the 1964 Gulf of Tonkin incident, previously secret naval communications indicated Saturday.
>
> Defense Secretary Robert McNamara disclosed that President Johnson had held up a bombing raid on North Vietnam in retaliation for a Communist torpedo boat attack on two U.S. destroyers until he was "damned sure what had happened."

When Goulden saw the rewritten story under *his* byline, he blew his stack and complained to managing editor Gillen. Gillen said there was nothing he could do about it. Goulden then wrote a letter to Annenberg himself: "For the record," he said, "I wish to disassociate myself from a grossly erroneous story . . . which appeared under my byline. The first paragraph of this story is without foundation in fact, and was not written in this bureau. . . . I do not wish to assume responsibility for inaccurate reportage which appeared in your columns under my name."

Annenberg never replied to Goulden and made no effort to inform *Inquirer* readers of the correct version of this important international incident.

∘ ∘ ∘

Incongruously, for a newspaper owned by a man appointed as an ambassador, it is in the sphere of world and international news that the *Inquirer* fell especially short. Although it didn't have a single staffer with any amount of foreign reporting experience anyway, its editors frequently evaluated such news through the perspective of Annenberg's political philosophy or international viewpoint. One hawkish U.S. senator, for instance, once made a speech on the floor of the Senate claiming that the United States was going to invade North Vietnam. Washington insiders, aware of the senator's penchant for publicity and his usual complete lack of accurate information, dismissed his claim immediately. The wire services gave his speech two short paragraphs. The *Inquirer* deskmen, however, planted the wire story atop a Vietnam wrap-up and topped it with huge page-one headlines.

Sometimes, however, *Inquirer* editors had only to make minor adjustments in wire-service pieces to reflect Annenberg's my-country-right-or-wrong attitude. One recent Associated Press photo, for instance, showed American soldiers pushing what the AP's original caption said were "Vietcong suspects, one of them a woman," toward a helicopter. When the photo appeared in the *Inquirer* the woman was cropped out of it and the suspect became a "Vietcong prisoner."

Actually, Annenberg's views on foreign policy had been difficult for his editors to keep abreast on. When they didn't verge on the simplistic, they tended to echo his favorite expert on the subject, Robert Strausz-Hupe, one of the original Cold Warriors and head of the University of Pennsylvania's Foreign Policy Research Institute before his nomination by Nixon as ambassador to Morocco. Strausz-Hupe wrote regularly for the *Inquirer,* almost always about the dangers of the Communist peril (he feels the so-called Sino-Soviet split may be a colossal hoax perpetrated by the Kremlin to further its aim of world domination), and his every utterance or speech was carried in full. ("Every time he farted we carried the entire text," recalls a former *Inquirer* deskman.)

The way the *Inquirer* played most of the daily news generally reflected indirect rather than direct control by Annenberg. On the other hand there were numerous occasions when the publisher himself directly interfered with his staff's attempt to do a legitimate job of news coverage. There were few nights that went by without his calling the assistant managing editor on duty to check the handling of running stories and, since the early "bulldog" edition was rushed to his home a half-hour after it was off the press, he would often take the opportunity to pull stories he didn't want given the extensive distribution of the *Inquirer*'s morning "Final." Once, for instance, two stories—one on the *Temple Free Press,* an underground paper, and the other on a black militant —were yanked when he discovered them in the first edition. He reportedly considered them "un-American."

However, he also directly prevented his own newsmen from covering news events because of personal interests. Once when he invited his close friend Ronald Reagan into town for a private dinner he gave specific orders that the California governor was not to be "bothered" by any of his reporters. The whole *Inquirer* news staff fumed in frustration the next day as they read the interview Reagan had granted *Bulletin* reporters at the airport.

Another illustrative incident involving Reagan occurred when the California governor was invited by Annenberg to speak at a $100-a-plate Republican fundraising dinner at Philadelphia's Convention Hall. When the dinner was picketed by a large group of welfare recipients and sympathetic supporters protesting the low level of public-assistance payments, *Inquirer* reporter Alfred Klimcke wrote a story which, in part, contrasted the "mink- and cashmere-clad" dinner guests arriving in their chauffeur-driven limousines to the gaunt and ragged welfare recipients handing out leaflets which said, "Not all God's children have shoes." In his story, Klimcke also depicted some of the dinner guests as coldly brushing hurriedly past the demonstrators with eyes kept straight ahead, and others as looking silly—

as when one picket "rushed to open the back door of an arriving limousine before the chauffeur could reach it and handed a leaflet to the smiling elderly matron who emerged. 'I'm so glad you're for Reagan,' the lady gushed."

Annenberg was furious when he read that. He demanded to know how the story had gotten into his paper (a young night deskman hadn't caught it), scribbled comments in red marking pencil all over a clipping of it, and sent down to executive city editor Morrie Litman for an explanation. Litman called Klimcke on the carpet and chewed him out. Klimcke protested that he had merely described what had happened outside Convention Hall as he saw it and that Annenberg had no right to complain about a legitimate news story. Litman turned red. "It's Annenberg's paper," he fumed at Klimcke, "and *he* can do what *he* wants with it!"

What Walter Annenberg most wanted to do with the *Inquirer* was to use it to help further his personal and social ambitions. As both incidents concerning his friend Ronald Reagan point out, it was much more important in Annenberg's mind that a certain amount of respect and deference be shown to his distinguished guest than it was that the *Inquirer* get a good news story. This attitude was especially manifest in Annenberg's direct orders restricting coverage of the 1968 presidential campaign. For one thing, he didn't like the way city editor Phil Schaeffer handled the news coming out of the Republican convention in Miami. He thought there was too much emphasis given to the activities of the dissidents and the militants trying to disrupt the affair. And he later had to pull, after he caught them in the first edition, a couple of columns he thought went beyond the bounds of propriety, one favorable to Rockefeller and the other critical of Agnew. Nixon's nomination gave him a direct stake in the results of the election, so Annenberg decided that the safest method to avoid embarrassment either way was simply not to have any direct coverage of the campaign at all. That's why he refused to assign *any* reporters to the candidates, an unprecedented omission for a major metropolitan newspaper, and ordered that all campaign news be taken directly from the wire services.

The fact is that well prior to the election the *Inquirer*'s news operation has increasingly reflected Annenberg's principal concern and interest, what he has called "the root issue" of crime and law enforcement. He is tremendously disturbed by "the spirit of desperation in our land" and disgusted with the "widespread desecration of every traditional ideal that would make patriotism a dirty word." He truly believes that many of the campus and black militants are being manipulated by Communists and that law enforcement has been hampered by "mealy-mouthed court decisions favoring the criminal."

One of Annenberg's favorite editorial cartoons, quite typical of the blaringly fatuous type the *Inquirer* seemed to prefer, appeared shortly after Nixon's election. It showed a square-jawed figure labeled "Hoover" wearing an "FBI" badge and standing in a guard post marked

"USA." A John Q. Public figure, pointing him out to his young daughter, is saying: "He's still on guard, honey—let's be thankful for that!"

In Annenberg's last months of control, the topic of law and order had been the subject of more editorials than any other in the *Inquirer* (though favorable comment about anything that President Nixon did ran a close second). And Annenberg's concern and attitude were specifically reflected in the *Inquirer*'s handling of news stories. Gang murders, holdups, and rapes got very big front-page coverage, usually backed by editorials calling for more support and money for the police department. And Annenberg seemed to be moving men up to key slots on the paper who share his thinking on the law-and-order issue. His most recent city editor, for instance, former *Daily News* staffer Henry Belinger, was an affable but tough newspaperman out of the tabloid school. "He got his idea of what a city editor should be from a 1928 movie," claims a deskman. A personable, well-liked guy, Belinger was also hiring and moving up staffers who see things his way. (One reporter who was quickly gaining status once asked Martin Luther King as he alighted from a plane in Philadelphia, "Is it true that the ultimate aim of your campaign is interracial marriage?")

One of the results of Annenberg's preoccupation with the law-and-order issue was the development of a close association with Philadelphia Police Commissioner Frank Rizzo. A big, burly, blue-jawed, quick-fisted cop (he has been involved in more assault and battery charges, filed both against him and by him, than any other city policeman) , Rizzo is the hero of the white backlashing bigots, the anathema of black militants, and the grudgingly respected peacekeeper of the moderates. It is Rizzo who will clamp a sort of martial law on Philadelphia if the racial violence he has kept capped for so long ever erupts. (He did exactly that in the hot summer of 1967, when it appeared that the city might blow, banning assemblies of more than a few people.) His reputation as one of the toughest cops in the nation is neither unfounded nor unearned.

Frank Rizzo got very special handling by the *Inquirer*'s news department. All of his pronouncements were given heavy play and his influence with the publisher had reached the point where simply by calling managing editor Gillen he could get a scheduled story killed, as he did do in at least once instance. A reporter, returning from covering a black protest meeting against Rizzo, asked the night city editor how much he should write on it. The reply: "Write all you want, nothing is going to be used." Rizzo, in fact, once told an *Inquirer* reporter directly: "If anything negative gets into your story, you'll be out looking for a new job tomorrow."

So close had Annenberg's relationship with Rizzo become that the publisher had begun to spend some evenings riding around with the police commissioner in his unmarked patrol car in order to get a close-up view of crime on the streets. Editorial after editorial supported the commissioner's cry for more money and manpower. And when the head of the Police Athletic League, a movie-house owner named Paul Klieman, offered Annenberg the chance to be the guest of honor at the second annual PAL dinner (the first guest of honor was Rizzo himself), Annenberg declined, but offered to donate $25,000 for a new youth center in South Philadelphia to be called the Frank Rizzo PAL Center. There were also rumors that Annenberg intended to push Rizzo for mayor of Philadelphia.

∘ ∘ ∘

The question is one of priorities. It is quite clear that Walter Annenberg subjugated the responsibility of the Philadelphia *Inquirer* to provide objective news coverage to his own subjective assessment of what is in the community's best interests. That's precisely why he can't quite understand why his motives should at all be questioned. There are indications, in fact, that he considers himself something of a martyr in this respect. A story he likes to tell, ostensibly in relation to his great philanthropic contributions, concerns his meeting with Winston Churchill. He was sitting next to the esteemed English statesman at a dinner and in the course of conversation told him how disappointed he had been with the British electorate for turning Churchill and his party out of office so soon after the war. Annenberg said it was difficult for him to believe that the English could have been so "ungrateful" in the light of Churchill having saved the empire. "Mr. Churchill chuckled," Annenberg recalls, "and put his hand on my shoulder and said: 'Look not for reward from others but hope that you have done your best.' "

Walter Annenberg says he will always remember those words, that they have had a "tremendous impact" on him. There is no doubt in his own mind that he tries to do what is best, that he has striven to be a man of courage and determination in the face of adversity and that he has always demonstrated a concern for the direction and welfare of his community and his country.

What Walter Annenberg hasn't done, however, is manifest an awareness that his role as publisher of one of the largest daily newspapers in the country transcended any personal assessment of his public responsibility as a wealthy or even politically influential individual.

He did not, in sum, show that he considers freedom of the press *the* most important element in the maintenance of an effective democracy, or that he really believes the ultimate role of an influential newspaper is to provide meaningful and objective coverage, untainted by personal prejudices or viewpoints and unlimited by special interests.

Walter Annenberg simply hasn't displayed the most crucial instinct of a good newspaperman, an unadulterated, consistent reverence for the truth.

"He doesn't know and has never known what a good newspaper should be," says a once-close associate, "and he had no one around him who will or could tell him."

Neither was he ever driven to the necessity of higher editorial standards by the competition from Philadelphia's other daily, the *Bulletin*. In fact, for the most part, the *Bulletin* pretended it was the *only* newspaper in Philadelphia, deliberately ignoring stories that *Inquirer* reporters may have hit upon. It even turned its head when the *Inquirer* publicly exposed its ace reporter as a black-mailer. And recently, when reports of a Philadelphian being named ambassador to the Court of St. James's first came through, it timidly picked up a news-service piece, as if fearful that any original reporting might reveal a competitive bias. In fact, the *Bulletin* even killed three columns about Annenberg by syndicated muck-raker Drew Pearson. (There may be hope for the *Bulletin* in the foreseeable future. As this was going to press there was a revamping of its editorial department with a new, young, and aggressive managing editor attempting a rejuvenation job on the Old Lady of Filbert Street.)

Nevertheless, in view of Annenberg's record of sub-verting the news operations of the *Inquirer,* the question that inevitably arises is whether he ever was, despite his own proclamations as such, a newspaperman at heart. Certainly his handling of the *Daily News* was another indication that editorial standards of excellence weren't given high priority in his thinking. When he bought the tabloid from Matt McCloskey for $3 million in 1957, Annenberg said: "We'll build the *News* into a solid prop-erty." He immediately cut its six editions down to two, held its locked pages on the presses until the *Inquirer* finished mopping up the morning market, and pushed its late edition up to compete with the firmly entrenched afternoon *Bulletin*. He also fired seventy-seven staffers and moved the paper's news operation into the Inquirer Building, where, according to one *News* veteran, an "instant hate" between staffs sprang up. Relegated to the status of a bastard child, the woefully undermanned *News* nevertheless tried to maintain its dignity as a sensation-seeking tabloid and, largely because it suffered from less direct interference from its owner than its sister publication, often did a far more aggressive and objective job on local reporting.

Yet despite his proclaimed determination after the death of his father to make the *Inquirer* one of the finest newspapers in the country, Walter Annenberg never instituted a progressive program to expand that paper's ability to do a better job of collecting and presenting the news. In fact, the reverse seems to be the case. Where once the *Inquirer* had correspondents scattered throughout Europe, and even one in Moscow, the extent of its "foreign" coverage deteriorated to two men in its Washington bureau, one in Harrisburg, and three in Camden. It rarely, if ever, sent a reporter abroad, with the exception of its fashion editor's annual sojourn in Paris. ("He gave a million dollars to the Israeli emergency relief fund," says one staffer, "but he wouldn't think of sending a reporter to Tel Aviv.") There were belt-tightening periods when a reporter had to get permission from his superior to make a long-distance call. A crucial United Nations debate had never been covered directly and even the *Inquirer* library was ordered to clip only local news items. Its "in-depth" background pieces and "news-analysis" wrap-ups on foreign affairs were written primarily from *The New York Times* index and national news-magazine sources. In the early days of American involvement in the Vietnam war, a former staffer with a Canadian passport offered to go to Hanoi, a coup that would have given the *Inquirer* an early, informative, and prestigious series of behind-the-enemy-lines reports. He was refused permission. And although more than 170 newsmen, many from relatively small, unaffluent papers across the country, accompanied President Nixon on his recent swing through Europe, the *Inquirer* was unrepresented. Annenberg seemed intent on running the *Inquirer* in the cheapest way possible.

Many years ago, a former top Triangle executive was chatting amiably one evening with Walter Annenberg when the publisher, in an easy, ruminative spirit, asked him what job, if he had a choice from within the entire organization, he would most prefer. The executive, who always thought he had a literary bent, said he would like to be an editor. Annenberg waved his hand deprecatingly. "Naah," he said. "Editors are a dime a dozen." Then he leaned forward and said seriously: "Learn *my* business."

In 1965, the respected publisher of Buenos Aires' *La Prensa*, Dr. Gainza Paz, made a speech in New York in which he said:

> We know the responsibility of all good editors: to stimulate reader interest in the progress and development of their country. We also know that we ought to find ways of awakening that interest, despite the fact that sometimes uninformed readers appear to be indifferent.
>
> We also know that newspapers should interpret the news without bias, and without fear of giving conflicting viewpoints. And most importantly . . . a paper

should express its own view clearly and without concern for the consequences.

But even beyond its duty to inform, beyond its editorial policy, no matter how courageous that may be, the true journalist must somehow create a bond of confidence between the readers and the newspaper. Only then can he expect to have their support in defense of a press freedom that guarantees the people's right to know.

The *Inquirer* certainly did not create that "bond of confidence" and, as a result, despite Annenberg's claim to be first and foremost a newspaperman, few would argue that he fits Dr. Paz's definition of a "true journalist." He has gotten numerous awards as a publisher, of course, including a French Legion of Honor citation for supporting the organization of a "France Forever" resistance group before World War II (ironic in view of the *Inquirer*'s eventually virulent anti-Gaullist stance). But one of the most interesting honors ever received by Annenberg was his selection as one of the recipients of the 1967 Pennsylvania Awards for Excellence.

Two things make that award especially significant: One is that it is given only to those Pennsylvanians who have achieved exceptional honor in their field. (Among those who have received it are baseball great Stan Musial, writer James Michener, and astronaut Charles Conrad, Jr.) The other is that although it was given to Annenberg in recognition of his achievement in the field of "Journalism," the citation avoided any mention of the *Inquirer*, said nothing about his journalistic ethics or standards, and circumvented the mention of any specific achievement as a newspaperman. Although the wording of the award was a bit circumlocutory, the essence of it was that Annenberg was being cited in the field of "Journalism" because of his philanthropy in that direction.

"The rise of the craft of journalism to its honored status as a profession," said the citation, "can be credited in a large part to the concern of individuals who have helped establish the educational facilities to train new practitioners of the Fourth Estate. Walter H. Annenberg . . . has demonstrated his response to this need in his role as founder of the Annenberg School of Communications of the Graduate School of the University of Pennsylvania. As a leading publisher and working editor in the field of American journalism, his sense of duty to the youth who will continue to uphold the standards set by today's newsmen is worthy of our admiration."

It *is* admirable that Annenberg feels this "sense of duty" toward youth. It would be even more admirable if he felt a keener responsibility to "uphold the standards" of American journalism those youth are supposed to follow. But that, of course, was especially difficult for a man who viewed editors as a commodity on the employment market worth no more than "a dime a dozen."

The summary effects of Annenberg's attitudes toward the editorial responsibilities of the *Inquirer* made themselves felt in a number of ways. Although it is one of the half-dozen largest morning newspapers in the country—and the third-ranking Sunday paper in ad lineage—its status among newspapermen was very low when Annenberg owned it. In a 1962 survey to determine which newspapers reporters in the nation's capital used in their work and which they considered fair and reliable, the *Inquirer* didn't show up in the resulting list of the top twenty. For years one of the most authoritative surveys of newspaper quality ranking has been taken by New York public-relations counsel Edward L. Bernays. He conducts a national poll of close to 1,600 daily-newspaper publishers, asking them to rank the nation's top newspapers using their own judgment and the unquestioned standards of journalism enunciated by such giants as Joseph Pulitzer and Adolph Ochs. Says Bernays: "In all the years I've taken the survey, I don't recall the *Inquirer* ever being mentioned."

During a New York newspaper strike, the editors of the *New Republic* commented: "You never fully realize how bad most American dailies are till you face a crisis like this. We have tried reading the Philadelphia *Inquirer,* a journal which contributes to the intellectual emaciation of that city. In a grab bag opposite the editorial page it squeezes together features and columnists, cut down to fit, lopping off the climax of a thoughtful Lippmann column the other day so that the rest of the article hardly made sense. No wonder *Time* and *Newsweek* find an audience."

It is also no wonder that after Walter Annenberg took over the operation of the *Inquirer,* there were few, if any, times when the staff of the newspaper felt a common pride in the product being produced. Annenberg's continuing interference in the efforts of most of his men to do a legitimate job of reporting and editing often created a deep sense of frustration. One evening, after a story about a narcotics raid was killed because the father of one of the high school students involved was a close friend of an associate of Annenberg, the night city editor began answering the telephone with: "Suppression Central here."

Said a recent edition of a *Newspaper Guild* bulletin about the working atmosphere at the *Inquirer:*

> Stagnation, alienation, disengagement—soft words with harsh overtones. In the crudest sense newspapers are conveyor belts for the dolors of their time. As newspapermen we record, and inevitably share, the discords swirling about us. How we do our job in this moment in history can be of more than passing significance.
>
> Primarily our concern as a union is wages, hours and welfare. But there are deeper aspects of our employment that also demand elaboration. They have a bearing on spirited newspapering, teamwork, loyalty, and above all—a redeeming sense of purpose. Such abstractions may be irrelevant in a sausage factory; on a newspaper they should be part of its lifeblood.

Within the last decade alone, turnover in the *Inquirer*'s city room has been estimated as high as 70 percent. Not long ago, resignations spurted to the point where a wag posted a notice on the city-room bulletin board: NO RESIGNATION ACCEPTED UNDER PENALTY OF DISMISSAL. "Thanks to Annenberg, it has become the type of news operation it is tough to respect," says a former editor.

"We were the only metropolitan newspaper in the country that got crank calls from our own reporters."

"The spirit of Annenberg hangs over this place," admitted one staffer, but a few weren't even willing to discuss the situation while Annenberg was boss. Said one in refusing: "I work for a vicious man, I can't take the chance of talking. I'm too old to go out looking for another job." There was a feeling that Annenberg had a basic lack of respect for those he employed. One of the most telling blows to morale ever suffered by any newspaper staff was the box, signed by "The Board of Editors" (a nonexistent entity), which accompanied the story revealing Harry Karafin's blackmailing activities. It asked readers of the *Inquirer* to come forward if they had "knowledge of any improper or unethical professional acts by any editorial employee."

While Walter Annenberg may reflect a measure of basic compassion in his generous record of charitable contributions and philanthropy, the fact that he directed such grossly insensitive acts against his own employees was indicative of his lack of real concern about what that Guild bulletin called "spirited newspapering." Far from unrelated was the sharp and repercussive blow to staff morale that occurred during the trial of blackmailer Karafin. In a desperate attempt to rationalize his own actions, Karafin, while in the witness box, smeared the names of some of his former fellow reporters by accusing them of accepting money for freelance jobs which he charged were in conflict with their journalistic responsibilities. The *Inquirer* dutifully printed all his unsubstantiated charges. Those whose names he mentioned angrily demanded that the *Inquirer* also print their answer to the charges. Managing editor Gillen told them that Annenberg said he would do so following the end of the trial. Later, however, when one of the staffers demanded that Annenberg keep that promise, he was told that the publisher had changed his mind.

That was the reason for another exodus of very good men from the *Inquirer*. Among those to go in this wave was Joe Goulden, a crack investigative reporter who had worked his way up to the coveted position of chief of the paper's Washington bureau. Goulden, too, was finally utterly disgusted with having been, as he put it, "impressed into so many lynch mobs in past years." In one last act of self-ablution, he wrote an explanation to Annenberg himself, concluding: ". . . and I am only now beginning to realize what a truly shabby bastard you are."

It seems almost tragic that the son of a man who was one of the best-liked employers of any publication, the heir determined to build a monument that would reflect honor on the memory of his father, should be considered in that way by even one employee.

In the box which accompanied its Karafin story, the *Inquirer*, plainly groping for a rationalization for its self-exposure, said: "A foundation stone of democracy is the awareness that man is fallible, that by his very nature he is susceptible to weaknesses and blindness, and that power and privilege do nothing to diminish those susceptibilities."

It is ironic that those same words might be relevant

to a propitious consideration of Walter Annenberg's character.

Nevertheless, Walter Annenberg can, if he prefers, consider the record of his relationship with the *Inquirer* merely as a part of a larger pattern of destiny to which he has been directing his life. He can, and perhaps justifiably so, view his tremendous and admirable philanthropic work, his impressive financial achievements, his reputation as the builder of a national communications empire, and his personal renown as a generous, warm, and gracious host to the most influential and powerful men in the world—he can view all of these as *the* significant measurements, the touchstones of his real legacy, that have culminated in his appointment to a post of international prestige. And certainly Walter Annenberg can, if he cares to, look upon that kind of achievement as reflecting the ultimate honor to his father's memory.

Moe Annenberg himself perhaps would have even considered his son's ambassadorial appointment a kind of prophetic purification of his own legacy. In his memoirs, published back in 1941, *Inquirer* supplement editor Emile Gauvreau recalled Moe Annenberg's significant role in the campaign of Arthur H. James during the 1938 Pennsylvania gubernatorial race:

> The publisher was confident of victory and discussed with gusto the political horizon which lay before us. He believed the country was headed for a Republican landslide in 1940 and that as the Governor of Pennsylvania, a strategic state in a national election, James, who preached budgets and who was beginning to talk

more and more like Coolidge every day, would have
an excellent chance of going to the White House. What
Moe would be in those great days to come was beyond
prediction. Perhaps he might begin by accepting an
appointment as Ambassador to the Court of St. James's.
I suggested this to "Fitz" [managing editor John J. Fitz-
patrick] during the battle, but he was too busy to laugh.

# Diplomatic Epilogue

The emergence of an intensely private man into the public arena naturally aroused much fascination. For sixty-one years of his life Walter Annenberg had, with his wealth and power, jealously guarded against invasions of his autocratic privacy. Having always displayed a thin-skinned sensitivity and a penchant for volatile reaction, he suddenly stepped into a job where both characteristics could be disastrous, not only for himself personally but also for the country he represented. His obsessive desire for public recognition and social acceptability cast him into the show-window worlds of diplomatic society and international politics, both of which are subject to the kind of critical press and public scrutiny Annenberg never relished and little tolerated. It would seem to necessitate a complete change in his style and methods of operation. Annenberg himself acknowledged that there would have to be at least one important change. "As an editor," he said, "I have become accustomed to an editorial page. I am simply going to have to operate without an editorial page." Then he stoically admitted: "This is going to be a matter of discipline, and a matter of discipline is indeed a very healthy condition for all citizens."

Nevertheless, because the man's name was Walter Annenberg, the question of how the new American ambassador to the Court of St. James's would fare burned with bright intensity right from the instant of its announcement.

Before the United States Senate Foreign Relations Committee had even held a hearing on Annenberg's nomination, nationally syndicated columnist Drew Pearson claimed that the announcement of the appointment was "standing British diplomacy on its ear." Said Pearson: "What has flabbergasted them is Annenberg's background. Not only is he divorced, and the Court of St. James's frowns at divorce, but the Annenberg fortune was built up by Chicago gang warfare." Nevertheless, Pearson predicted, Committee chairman J. William Fulbright would probably treat Annenberg rather gingerly at his hearing for fear of interrupting his "honeymoon" with the administration. "Other members of the Senate Foreign Relations Committee are also loath to tangle with a powerful newspaper publisher [who] has shown every disposition to throw the weight of his publishing empire against anyone who opposes him," said the columnist. "They know how vindictive publisher-ambassador Annenberg can be."

Annenberg was introduced to the Senate committee by Pennsylvania senator Hugh Scott. In his sixteen years as a United States representative and his eleven years as a senator, Scott had never been without the editorial support of the Philadelphia *Inquirer*. He introduced Annenberg to the committee as "a person of competence and a broad range of vision and intelligence, tact and diplomatic skill."

Prior to the actual questioning of Annenberg, Chairman Fulbright (who would later probe the appointee more critically than Pearson predicted) made the rather unprecedented admission that the hearing itself was an impotent exercise. "As you know," he told Annenberg, "under the traditions of the Senate a nominee for an ambassadorial post, as a practical matter, is never rejected once it is made public and formal."

Although the committee took far more than twice as much time with Annenberg as it did with Jacob Beam, the nominee for ambassador to Russia, *and* John Eisenhower, the nominee to Belgium, both of whom it questioned the same day, the session was in no way an attempt to probe or reveal the depth of the man's character or his potential ability to handle the job. Both Senator Clifford Case of New Jersey and Senator Jacob Javits of New York praised Annenberg highly, and both admitted they were close personal friends of his. ("His answers are completely reliable," testified Case.) Senator George Aiken of Vermont conducted him through a recitation of some of his citations and awards, including the medal he received from Finland because he purchased newsprint there when it was trying to re-establish the industry after World War II.

Senator John Sparkman did raise some interesting questions about possible conflicts of interest. Annenberg said he had discussed that with the legal adviser of the State Department and that he was prepared to resign from the boards of all the public corporations on which he sat and to put into trusteeship all securities in which he held a beneficial interest. Sparkman then asked: "Did he say that that would clear up any questions of a conflict of interest?" Said Annenberg: "Yes, with the possible exception that we discussed the editorial-page direction of my newspapers, and I indicated that I would, of course, abstain for the term of my service from any direction of the editorial page or pages."

Annenberg, however, carefully avoided mentioning how much of a role he would continue to play in the editorial direction of the *Inquirer*'s news operation. That, of course, was how he had most effectively used the power of his newspaper, but Sparkman was either unaware of that or chose not to pursue it.

There was no indication that the committee or its staff had done any significant independent investigating into Annenberg's background. The sharpest questions, asked by Chairman Fulbright, were all based on information that had appeared in Drew Pearson's syndicated columns. Pearson, for instance, had said that Annenberg had been "a loyal and generous supporter of Richard Nixon." When Fulbright asked him about it, Annenberg stated flatly: "I made no contributions to the Nixon campaign." Later in the hearing, however, when questioned in more detail, Annenberg admitted that his wife did make a fat donation to Nixon's political coffers, as well as to Senator Hugh Scott's.

Fulbright also brought up a few other matters mentioned in Pearson's columns, but in many ways it seemed an attempt to cover some very delicate ground for the record without probing or kicking up anything that might arouse an outcry by the press or public against the nomination. His questions, for instance, about the *Inquirer*'s ruthless hatchet job which Annenberg ordered against Pennsylvania gubernatorial candidate Milton Shapp were an example. When asked about it, Annenberg admitted that he considered Shapp "an irresponsible individual," adding indignantly: "Mr. Shapp attempted to run for the governorship on the basis of denouncing the Pennsylvania Railroad."

"Well," said Fulbright, not completely tongue in cheek, "that is close to blasphemy in Philadelphia, isn't it?"

Fulbright, however, failed to press the question of Annenberg's sense of propriety or his awareness of the conflict of interest involved in sanctioning *Inquirer* editorials which denounced Shapp for his opposition to the rail merger without revealing the publisher's massive financial interest in the Pennsylvania Railroad.

Neither did Fulbright, in raising questions about the original source of his fortune and the facts about his father's jail sentence, press Annenberg for details about the extent of his involvement in the tax-evasion case. Annenberg, in fact, handled that area of questioning rather well and aroused an expression of compassion from the committee chairman himself. His father's imprisonment, he said, was "a tragedy in the life of the family," but it had eventually become a source of positive inspiration for him. "There is," he explained, "no question that a tragedy of such a magnitude will either destroy you or inspire you to overcome it and drive you on to deeds of affirmative character."

"I think that is a very appropriate comment," said Fulbright.

Another matter was touched upon rather lightly by Fulbright which, if probed in depth, might have revealed something about the ambassadorial candidate's intellectual grasp of the complex economic, social, and political factors which govern a nation's foreign policy.

Following General de Gaulle's efforts to assert France as the leader of Europe's destiny, Annenberg had not only produced a series of bitingly critical editorials in the *Inquirer*; he had also spent a good deal of money to reprint the editorials as paid advertisements in newspapers in Canada, London, and Brussels.

Fulbright asked him why he had gone through so much trouble to attack the French leader. Because, said Annenberg, after all the money that the United States had given France as aid after the war, he considered General de Gaulle's policy "the very essence of ingratitude."

The only time Fulbright came close to getting Annenberg sweating a bit—forced him, in fact, into dissembling

—was when he brought up an incident which occurred after the death of Annenberg's favorite Pennsylvania Supreme Court justice, Michael Musmanno.

Was it true, asked Fulbright, that he had instructed an editor in writing the obituary to attribute part of the responsibility for Musmanno's death to his long-time political foe Senator Joseph Clark?

"Untrue," said Annenberg.

"And the paper did not do any such thing?" asked Fulbright.

"Not to my recollection," said Annenberg.

The facts are that Annenberg had specifically insisted to managing editor John Gillen—*in the presence of another editor*—that Musmanno's obituary note that one of the "probable causes" of his death was the "terrible maligning" he had taken from political opponent Clark. As previously noted, it never got into the *Inquirer* because Annenberg, despite being so adamant initially, changed his mind after Gillen strongly argued against such editorializing in news columns.

Annenberg had obviously long ago sensed he was going to be on thin ice in this area. He had always backed Musmanno in his repeated attempts to knock Clark out of his U.S. Senate seat, and although Clark was defeated by an aggressive young congressman named Richard Schweiker after Musmanno died, Annenberg knew that Clark's influence in the Senate was considerable. Annenberg became especially concerned after he learned that he was going to have to appear before the Senate Foreign Relations Committee as an ambassadorial nominee.

Clark had been a ranking member of that committee. So Annenberg made it a point at his hearing to tell the committee that he had recently spoken to Clark at a luncheon in Philadelphia. "Senator Clark came up to me," he beamed, "and said he wanted to express his great gratitude because I completely abstained from any adverse editorial comment in relation to him in the last campaign."

What Annenberg didn't tell the committee was that he had deliberately but rather quietly gone out of his way to smooth his relationship with Clark immediately after he learned he was going to be named ambassador to England. He sent a reporter to Clark to tell him that the *Inquirer* wanted to do an upbeat piece about the former senator in retirement. Clark caught the ball. "Tell Walter not to worry," he told the reporter. "I won't try to stop his appointment."

In sum, then, the Senate Foreign Relations Committee made no real attempt to discover for itself or reveal to the public the complex nature of the man who was going to represent the United States in an important diplomatic post. Its members could not tell, from either the official information available or the results of the hearing at any rate, just how effective an ambassador Annenberg would be. Annenberg himself, however, might have hinted at his own view of the job when he volunteered that he was going to make two important changes (although he didn't indicate that he considered them *the* pressing priorities).

"I am desirous of refurbishing the Embassy residence,"

he said, "which from information that I have is in some real need of refurbishing, and I hastily want to add that in no sense do I want to be critical of Ambassador Bruce, who has been a tremendously effective representative of our country, but there does come a period when refurbishing is the order of the day."

(Chairman Fulbright, a former Rhodes Scholar and well aware of the high esteem in which the British held David Bruce, commented with a hint of cynicism: "Well, I didn't realize Ambassador Bruce would allow the Embassy to deteriorate.")

There was one other "radical change" that Annenberg said he would make as ambassador. "I happen to personally find the eagle that overhangs the Embassy office building on Grosvenor Square rather insensitive," he said, "and well do I remember when it was originally installed there was a hue and cry of resentment in Britain over that. I happen to agree with that because I found the enormity of that eagle rather blatant." Annenberg said he would probably "eliminate" the eagle.

The Senate Foreign Relations Committee voted, as Fulbright predicted it would, to confirm Annenberg's nomination as ambassador to England. There was only one dissent, and that was Chairman Fulbright's. It was later reported, however, that two members of the committee, instead of answering affirmatively when polled, merely said, "Present."

A few days later, the Senate itself approved Annenberg's appointment. Senator Stephen Young, a Democrat from Ohio, cast the only negative vote. "I cannot fathom the reason for our President nominating Mr. Annenberg to this extremely important and prestigious ambassadorial post," he said. Only Senator George Murphy, the former movie actor from California, spoke in favor of Annenberg's nomination. He had attended the same prep school as the publisher.

There was no doubt that Walter Annenberg considered his appointment the apex of his career. "It is indeed about as high an honor as any citizen could be offered," he said, and marched off to his new post in a surge of pomp and optimism. The night before his departure his very close friend, Lieutenant General Milton Baker, who runs Valley Forge Military Academy, arrived at Annenberg's Wynnewood estate with six busloads of polished cadets and, to the military roll of the drum and the blare of the trumpet, escorted the new ambassador through a beplumed and besashed column of honor guards as a sort of departing salute. (A photograph of the "surprise" ceremony later appeared in the *Main Line Times*.) And the next morning a special police detail ordered by Commissioner Frank Rizzo was on hand at Philadelphia International Airport to wave adieu as Annenberg's jet took off into the blue. It was a triumphant farewell for the man who had long aspired to such social and international prestige.

Walter Annenberg immediately had himself listed on the masthead of the Philadelphia *Inquirer* as "Editor and Publisher on leave of absence." And there were some minor changes in the operation of the newspaper. Aging executive editor E. Z. Dimitman, long Annenberg's liaison with the editorial side, went on a long cruise, took ill shortly after his return, spent some time in the hospital, and gradually became a less influential force on the paper. New city editor Harry Belinger tackled the news operation with the efficiency of an experienced deskman. Nevertheless, it was more than obvious that Walter Annenberg's hand still lay heavily on the *Inquirer*'s operation. No statement or pronounced policy of President Nixon went editorially unpraised and its strong law-and-order bias was still apparent in both its news and editorial columns.

Most Americans, however, hardly noticed that Walter Annenberg had left the country. They hardly noticed—and cared less—that they had a new ambassador representing them in the Court of St. James's. And yet it wasn't something that was unworthy of their concern, as Senator Fulbright himself indicated when he welcomed the appointee's appearance before his committee: "Mr. Annenberg," he had said, "the post to which you have been nominated is considered by many people, including myself, as the number one diplomatic post of our Foreign Service. You will be considered not only the President's representative but the representative of all of us because Great Britain is, in a sense, our mother country. I think the British and Europeans will look upon you, the ambassador, as representing the finest traditions of American society. You will be considered by foreigners as representing in a measure those qualities which have made America rich and powerful."

In most instances it is quite unusual for a foreign ambassador in any country to achieve any bit of notoriety that would bring him to the attention of anyone outside the diplomatic or governmental circles. Walter Annenberg wasn't in London very long when there appeared indications that he had achieved the unusual. An Englishwoman named Caroline Darby-Patterson was perturbed enough about it to write a letter to *Philadelphia Magazine.*

"I have recently arrived home after a very pleasant stay in Philadelphia," she wrote, "and during my stay I read with particular interest the issues of your magazine concerning the newly appointed American Ambassador to the Court of St. James's." She went on to point out that most ambassadors in England are not paid much attention by either the British press or public "unless they hold glittering parties or have an exceptionally beautiful wife or daughter." She found, she said, that most of her friends did not know very much about Walter Annenberg when he first arrived in London other than what they had read about his associations with Philadelphia and President Nixon and a bit about his family background. "Everyone felt that he was an unlikely choice but were not really that interested," she wrote.

But that, however, quickly changed, according to Miss Darby-Patterson. Stories were soon circulating and gossip flying about some of the antics and actions of the new American ambassador, she said, and many of her friends were beginning to laugh up their sleeves. The final straw for her came when she read an item about the American producer of *The Untouchables* being in London to arrange for two English script writers to do a television series about "the misadventures of a rather inept and incompetent American Ambassador to Britain." Assurances have been given, said Miss Darby-Patterson, that the character around whom the series will revolve bears no similarity whatsoever to persons living or dead. "But," she added, "most people here feel that no prizes need to be given for guessing who the inspiration for the series had been."

And that particularly perturbed Miss Darby-Patterson. "America's new Ambassador to England has become a joke and is a disaster to America's image in Britain," she wrote. "I am half American (my mother was born and bred in Philadelphia) and I feel particularly sensitive to the fun that is being made of Mr. Annenberg at the expense of the American people. Nobody can blame the British people for their justifiable mockery of this man, but surely out of all the great people in America, the country responsible for sending man to the moon, you could find some person more fitting to represent your country at the Court of St. James's."

Coincidentally, the editor of *Philadelphia Magazine* received another letter shortly afterward, this from a freelance writer in Donegal, Ireland, a man who knew a story brewing when he smelled one. "If you send a man to Fleet Street for a few weeks," he suggested, "you might get a grand follow-up on Walter the Ambassador. I was in London recently for a spell and heard quite a few stories about Walter and his antics in British circles. I have also seen one or two kooky pics of him riding in a fancy barouche with nag. Very protocol. The Annenbergs seem determined to show their wealth, which just isn't done in England. Because of diplomatic relations the ordinarily candid British press has laid off, but I'm sure your man could pick up some stuff to interest the folks back home."

As unlikely as it would seem, in a few short months on his new post Walter Annenberg appeared to be stirring comment enough to reach the remote corners of the British Isles. Hints of what was happening began floating back to the United States and, eventually, as knowledge-able an insider as *The New York Times*'s James Reston was moved to comment. Writing in his syndicated column, he ticked off a list of what he considered President Nixon's "avoidable blunders." Topping the list: "He didn't have to appoint Walter Annenberg, of all people, to be his Ambassador to London, of all places." (He later added: "The British expect us to be clumsy and Annenberg merely seems to confirm all their preju-dices about our political immaturity.")

Of course, it will be some time before any serious evaluation in depth can be made of Walter Annenberg in his role as ambassador to England. Although President Nixon appointed him the January after his election and the Senate confirmed him in March, Annenberg delayed his departure for London until late in April. Thereafter, for business or personal reasons, he made a number of trips back to the United States, including one for a few weeks' stay at his palatial California retreat and some golfing with President Nixon (which led consumer advo-cate Ralph Nader to complain: "President Nixon has spent more time with Ambassador Annenberg than with consumer advocates. That may be because consumer advocates don't usually play golf—Ambassador Annenberg does."). Thus even in the first six months on the job Annenberg didn't spend enough time working at it to permit any extensive study of how effective he was as an envoy. Besides, what marked influence, if any, his tenure will have on long-term British-American relationships— or even perhaps on foreign policy in general—will probably not be subject to valid evaluation until long after Annenberg is comfortably ensconced back in his baronial Palm Springs abode. Yet it is not without significance— if only in relation to what Senator Fulbright pointed out —that Annenberg was able to so quickly stir up as much comment in England as he has.

Granted, Annenberg himself could little help the fact that not everyone in England had been waiting for him with bells a-jangling. There was, naturally, some resentment at Nixon's not considering Britain worthy of an ambassador with professional credentials and a chestful of battle ribbons from the major diplomatic arenas of the world. Not that the English weren't used to ambassadors who were millionaires first and diplomats second, third, or fourth. Whiskey tycoon Joseph Kennedy was certainly far from the epitome of pin-striped finesse, while publisher John Hay (Jock) Whitney had a bit more polish but little more skill. Nevertheless, resentment at Annenberg's appointment seemed sharper than usual. The *New Statesman,* a strongly liberal periodical, complained: "If President Nixon had a sense of humour, he might have conceived of the designation of Walter Annenberg to be ambassador in London as a monstrous impractical joke. . . . But a good laugh is the last thing from the President's mind these days, and one can only conclude that the Annenberg appointment is either an expression of despair about America or contempt towards Britain." Andrew Kopkind, the *New Statesman*'s Washington correspondent added: "The Philadelphia press tycoon is no doubt a man of many qualities, but two in particular qualify him for America's 'premier diplomatic post': a loud editorial mouth and an enormous amount of money."

London's *Daily Express* quoted an English diplomat who, when informed of Annenberg's appointment, asked: "Is this Mr. Nixon's idea of how to get even with London for the Freeman appointment?" (England's ambassador to Washington, John Freeman, had, prior to his appointment, often been highly critical of Nixon even before he was elected President, but Freeman had been named to his post prior to Nixon's victory.)

Nevertheless, most of the British press initially remained tactfully noncommittal in a stiff-upper-lip sort of way. One paper, probably as a result of learning that he had something to do with horses, described Annenberg as a "sportsman." The *Daily Mail*, in a flash of hallucinatory optimism, somehow saw a speck of light in the dark, cavernous mystery of Annenberg's appointment: AMBASSADORS DON'T OFTEN COME AS COLORFUL AS THIS, it headlined one story. "Mr. Nixon has done us proud," said the front-pager. "We are going to get an American Ambassador who owns the country's top racing sheet, has a private army, a private golf course and seven sisters who are all multi-millionairesses. . . . The appointment of Walter H. Annenberg is an inspired one, which at least refutes those people who say Richard Nixon has a flair for being dull." Its even wilder conclusions: "Well, look at it this way, career diplomats have their worth. But Ambassadors like Walter Annenberg are fun."

The problem, from the British press's point of view, was that they were faced with a man about whom very little was known. A few newspapers attempted to have American correspondents interview him prior to his arrival in England, but Annenberg, characteristically, made himself unavailable. Mabel Elliott, the enterprising correspondent of the *Sunday Telegraph*, did manage to corner the charming and outspoken Leonore Annenberg, who immediately attempted to establish a bit of diplomatic rapport by praising a British product. "We haven't yet decided whether to take our private plane to London," Miss Elliott reported her as saying, "but we are definitely having our Rolls-Royce shipped over. It is by far the favourite and we feel lost without it." (Commented one Britisher: "Well, when we read that we all fell madly in love with the dear girl. Naturally, every Englishman feels *exactly* the same way about *his* Rolls.")

An interesting point is that the American community in London—and in particular its press corps—made no attempt to polish their fellow American's image prior to his arrival. "We did not stand up and applaud," was the way one correspondent put it. "Annenberg didn't exactly step into a cordial atmosphere," admitted another. "I guess we were all just waiting for him to fall flat on his face and all our British associates sensed our attitude."

That sort of comment, however, is made in retrospect and with an awareness of the fact that Annenberg, shortly after his arrival, appeared quickly to fulfill expectations. An expatriate from Annenberg's own hometown, a prominent advertising executive who has lived and worked in London for more than a decade, shook his head disconsolately when asked about the new ambassador: "He seems determined to live up to the image of the rich, gross, insensitive ugly American," he said. "I sometimes find myself apologizing for him."

It is not common for a newcomer to arrive in a country and become something of an instant national celebrity. Partially by the dint of circumstance, the new American ambassador managed to do just that. The occasion was the showing of a television program called *The Royal Family*. Co-produced by Independent Television and the British Broadcasting Company, the historic documentary was the first behind-the-scenes look at the daily life of the Queen and her family. It just happened that during the filming of this important show, Walter Annenberg presented his credentials to Her Royal Highness and thus became a part of it.

Too big a part, the way it turned out. Because of the significance of the program—a landmark in the centuries of monarchical rule—it was highly promoted throughout the country. There were very few television sets anywhere in the British Isles which were not tuned to it on the night of its initial showing, which took place less than two months after Annenberg had arrived in England. And those who missed it then were later given two additional opportunities to catch it on repeat showings. (It was also later obtained by the CBS television network and shown in the United States.) The program was expected to eventually reach 350 *million* viewers throughout the world. It would have been an excellent opportunity for the new American ambassador to display the proper diplomatic finesse his critics were claiming he lacked.

A good deal is lost in the mere verbal description of what happened. Annenberg is shown arriving at Buckingham Palace in a horse-drawn gilded coach as the narrator somberly explains: "All over the world the reception of ambassadors is extremely formal. This is to make sure they are all treated exactly the same." Annenberg, splendidly attired in formal white tie and silk top hat, descends from the coach and is greeted by an entourage of royal aides. Looking a bit lost, he is led inside and up a flight of steps to a reception room, where one of the aides suggests that he remove his hat. He is then given, in exquisite detail, the time-honored formula for presenting his credentials to the Queen. "And when the doors open we all take a pace forward with our *left* foot," instructs the chief protocol aide. "With our *left* foot," Annenberg dutifully repeats. Then comes the presentation itself. The huge oak doors swing open, and there in the center of the room, in all her regal splendor and finery, stands the Queen. "The American ambassador, Your Majesty," announces an echoing voice. Annenberg walks forward, bows stiffly, and in a slow, very deep and starchy *March*

*of Time*-like voice says: "Your Majesty, I have the honor
to present the letter of recall of my predecessor and my
own letters of credence." The Queen smiles politely.
"Thank you very much, indeed," she says softly as she
accepts his credentials. Then very casually and informally
she asks, "You aren't living at the Embassy at the moment, are you?" It is a simple enough question but Annenberg seems a bit stunned by it. He blinks, says "Uhhh,"
recovers, tucks in his chin, and stiffly intones: "We're in
the Embassy residence, subject, of course, to some of the
discomfiture as a result of a need for, uh, elements of
refurbishing and rehabilitation."

The Queen's reaction is interesting. She cocks her head
ever so slightly, flicks a puzzled eyebrow, and stands there
for a split moment with a bewildered expression on her
face. Then she quickly recovers, obviously decides she
perhaps had better get on with the formalities, and asks
the ambassador to present his staff.

There was a press preview of the program in a large
theatre one evening prior to its public telecasting. It
seemed as if every newspaperman in England was there.
"The whole theatre just erupted into horse laughs," recalls an American correspondent. "You sort of felt like
hanging your head."

For days afterward, the program was the talk of the
town, and probably all of England, with Annenberg's
performance the amusing highlight of almost every discussion. The *Sunday Telegraph* did rub it in a bit: "The
curious feature of this diplomatic event—and it is only
fair to say that Mr. Annenberg had taken a battering

from precise courtiers before he mauled the language so
—is that His Excellency still believes that he carried the
whole thing off in jaunty fashion. His Californian wife
agrees. 'The ambassador did beautifully,' she declared."

But the English are basically a compassionate people
and when the guffawing subsided many began expressing
their sympathy. "I feel bloody sorry for him," one government official said. "It could have happened to any of
us." Another reaction was later summed up by the television critic of the London *Sun* after the repeat showing
of the program:

"I missed it first time around (and was left out of all
conversations for a week), but I caught the second showing of the Royalty film and was absolutely mesmerized by
it.

"Now, though, the mesmer has lifted. My second
thoughts are not at all comfortable. . . . A much bigger
question (with possible backlash) is whether it was prudent to show the American Ambassador in such a merciless light.

"It was, I grant, an irresistible scene. The funniest
thing in the show. *Awful* in a way that no scriptwriter
could equal. I will be ever grateful to the Queen for letting us share it. But I wonder. . . .

"If it had been a one-go TV documentary for home
consumption only, that would have been one thing. The
poor American Ambassador's agony would have been
seen once, laughed at, and forgotten. It would have been
a private British joke. The biggest in-joke in the world.

"But it is not like that. This film is going all over the

world—including America. It will be shown time and
again. It will be seen by millions of people. Not everybody in the world has a British sense of humour. Not
everybody is as sophisticated as the British. . . ."

He suggested that the scene should have been cut from
the documentary in the interest of maintaining satisfactory British-American relationships.

If it hadn't been for Annenberg's television appearance, British reaction to his presence might not have been
on such a grand scale. Yet it still might have come about
as a result of a number of other incidents which contributed to the general impression he made shortly after
arriving in the country.

His very first speech, in fact, raised many an eyebrow.
It was, in the tradition of all maiden speeches by a newly
arrived American ambassador, presented before the Pil-
grims, a group of very top men in government, business,
and society whose avowed purpose it is to strengthen
Anglo-American relationships. Meetings of the group are
always nonpolitical, and those who speak before it take
the occasion to reinforce some positive aspect of mutual
interest in American or British affairs.

Not Annenberg. To the puzzlement of his distinguished audience, he tore into the "revolutionaries" behind the student riots in America and painted a vivid
picture of rifle-toting collegians turning campuses into
armed camps of disorder and turmoil. He also went out of
his way to praise his close friend Ronald Reagan, the
strongly conservative governor of California, for the determination and methods he has used to squash student

"insurrection" in his state. (Tear gas was dropped from helicopters at one Berkeley demonstration.)

As Annenberg spoke, his audience sat in stunned silence, and mustered only a bare ripple of applause when he was finished. The next day the British press termed his speech, among other things, "a surprising public debut." Wrote one bewildered observer: "It is almost unknown for an ambassador to make a swinging attack on his fellow-countrymen to a foreign audience." Another frankly called the speech "inept" and said that "it brought out all the Right-of-the-line prejudices of the rich American."

Annenberg was early criticized for blundering in other areas as well. *The Diplomatist*, an exclusive journal that chronicles the currents and undercurrents of the *corps diplomatique*, accused him of "queue cutting" in presenting his credentials to the Queen; that is, breaking precedence by jumping ahead of three other ambassadors who should have gone before him. In fact, because the presenting of credentials itself establishes the order of precedence—and precedence is the *modus dictum* of the diplomatic corps—the publication felt no compunction in letting Annenberg know exactly where he stood, in spite of his tactless tactic: "Still, it is believed to be the first time that an Ambassador having presented credentials to Her Majesty is below in precedence to others who have presented credentials to Her Majesty later than him."

Furthermore, said *The Diplomatist*, Annenberg departed from form in another matter: "He took with him to the Palace for the presentation of credentials his mar-

ried daughter, Wallis, who was introduced to Her
Majesty. Children of Ambassadors are not usually allowed
to accompany their parents for presentation of credentials. Even less so married children. In the Court Circular
no mention was made of daughter Wallis. The circular
kept to established rules even though the ceremony did
not."

That caused a bit of an initial stir among the members of the diplomatic corps but probably would not have
had a lasting effect on the new American ambassador's
relationships with them. As the months went by, however, it became apparent that Annenberg was making no
special effort to establish any such relationships. While
a good part of the life of the *corps diplomatique* revolves
around an endless series of cocktail parties and receptions,
it is at such informal gatherings that confidences are ex-
changed and close friendships made which could have a
profound effect on a country's foreign affairs. Annenberg
did not seem to be aware of this and *The Diplomatist*, as
the unofficial voice of the corps, was again forced to chide
him:

"Amongst the leading members of the diplomatic corps
in London," it editorialized, "there were many who complained about a certain aloofness in His Excellency's
predecessor, the Hon. David K. Bruce. This aloofness,
they said, was more than compensated by that Ambassador's experience and personal charm. The diplomats
who complained about Mr. Bruce were looking forward
to appreciating the new Ambassador's bluff and un-
pompous attitude. They have been deeply disappointed

so far. He has been even more unobtainable than his predecessor. To most he is still persona incognita. He has failed to attend a great many social functions where he could have been expected to come and so far has refused to mix with the bulk of the diplomatic corps in the same friendly, open and winning way as his opposite number from the other super-power, H.E. the Soviet Ambassador, Mr. M. Smirnovsky."

Neither was there any indication in his first several months on the job that Annenberg was making an effort to meet a cross section of British Government representatives. "Well, so far he has been a non-entity," admitted one prominent Member of Parliament. "We still see more of his predecessor than we do of him." Then, displaying a measure of diplomacy himself, he quickly added: "Not that we think he's anti-social at all. We all realize he's had a bit of a problem settling in and we're all looking forward to meeting him one of these days. We're very tolerant and we really do want to welcome ambassadors from abroad."

Some members of the diplomatic corps and many more members of the British Government itself, however, were less concerned with Annenberg's lack of mixing than they were with the circles he seemed interested in mixing in. "Those who have studied the form sheets," said one such observer, "have found that he has thus far pretty much been keeping rather aristocratic company, which makes many of us feel that's what *he* thinks makes England tick. That's not the case, of course, and it doesn't make a very good impression. There's naturally a resentment against anyone who attempts to cultivate the higher social strata or who is anxious only to move among the nobility. Unfortunately, the feeling now is that is what Annenberg is aiming at."

What helped reinforce that feeling was the exhibition that Annenberg arranged for thirty-two of his paintings at the posh Tate Gallery, a haut monde estuary. Scheduled eventually to hang in his Regency Park mansion, the paintings were shipped from his Wynnewood home outside Philadelphia and consisted, for the most part, of costly French Impressionist and Post-Impressionist works. When they saw them, London's art enthusiasts were awed. "U.S. Ambassador Walter Annenberg has added his name to the patrons of the dazzling world of London art exhibitions," reported Reuters. "The number of masterpieces within the exhibition's compact range startled art critics at the preview showing."

While the paintings were praised individually, some took the collection as a reflection of something about Annenberg's character. *Evening Standard* art critic Ian Dunlop commented: "Without wishing to detract anything from these pictures, it is worth saying that it is the sort of collection which only money can buy—and by money one means something in the order of 10 million dollars. . . . The impressive side of Mr. Annenberg's collecting has been his determination to go for best examples of an artist's output. He does not appear to have wasted money on trifles and stop-gaps; at least, if he has, they are not shown at the Tate. His argument must have been that if you have the money and you want a Cezanne you

might as well get a landscape of Mont Sainte-Victoire. . . .
Mr. Annenberg appears not only to have gone for the
best, but two of the best of everything. As a result, his
collection is curiously lacking in taste, by which I mean
bias. . . ."

"I think the collection," said another critic, "bespoke
the approach of an undiscriminating rich man, much like
the late J. P. Morgan's wine cellar."

How Annenberg took to functioning within the American embassy itself is another matter. To probe the
labyrinthine corridors of any Foreign Service operation
is risky and, to judge the validity of any expressed individual reactions, nearly impossible. Former Foreign
Service Officer William A. Bell recently wrote: "The
usual defensive explanation for Milquetoastian behavior
on the part of individual Foreign Service Officers is the
promotion system. FSO's are fond of describing it as a
high-rise outhouse, constructed so that each person—except for those at the very bottom—is subject to deposits
from those above but can deposit in kind upon those below. Although this is hyperbole, this general view of the
system is widely shared within the Department. Whether
it is accurate or not, belief in its validity creates a formidable operating reality; it hardly encourages dissent with
one's superior."

A number of members of the American Embassy in
London reported they were delighted with the manner
in which the new ambassador was handling his job.
Others wouldn't talk about it. ("I wouldn't touch that
subject with a forty-foot pole," said one officer when

called for comment, and quickly slammed down the telephone.) Most staffers on the lower echelons were delighted when Annenberg retreated from the proposal he had made to remove the huge spread-winged eagle from atop the building. They knew that much of the early British reaction against it had come about as a result of the thirty-five-long piece of gilded statuary having rested on street level for weeks prior to its being hoisted into place. They themselves had come to hold the big bird in a measure of endearment (poems had even been written about it) and were pleased when Annenberg made a peace pact with the eagle. "As long as he don't bother me," he agreed, "I won't bother him."

One top embassy insider who was willing to comment claimed that Annenberg may, in fact, turn out to be a more effective ambassador than his predecessor. While David Bruce was enormously popular with the British, his own staff was continually irked by his method of operating chiefly on his own level of diplomacy, often without keeping his assistants fully informed of what he was doing. "Annenberg seems anxious to make more effective use of his staff," this official said. "He is obviously a very able administrator, a very direct no-nonsense type who always knows exactly what he wants and, when he doesn't, finds out quickly enough." He was impressed with Annenberg's capacity for hard work, the long hours he was putting in and the sandwich lunches he insisted on having at his desk. He felt that the new ambassador was very eager to learn.

He had, it seemed, quite a lot to learn. "We were

shocked when he first arrived," admitted an unusually candid embassy staffer. "He seemed to know almost nothing about European affairs and had just a superficial knowledge of what we term the 'special relationship' between England and the United States." It was Annenberg's reply to a query about that "special relationship" which sent a member of the House of Lords rocking on his heels. The very proper Englishman asked the new ambassador his thoughts about it shortly after being introduced to him at a reception. Annenberg said he endorsed the concept of such a relationship completely, adding: "I have always maintained that England and America belong in bed together."

Annenberg, in his early months on the job at any rate, seemed determined to reinforce the English stereotype of Americans as rather blunt, straightforward characters not often given to the delicate approach. On one occasion, while dining at Pimlico's swank Thameside River Club, his eyes happened to alight on a Toulouse-Lautrec painting high on the wall. He immediately called for the maître d'hôtel and demanded: "Tell me about that painting, how did it get there?" He paused, then added suspiciously, "One of my friends in Philadelphia owns it." The maître d' calmly explained that it was merely a very good copy by French painter Jean Claude Latil, one of fifteen he had officially been commissioned to paint.

There were other early incidents which also aroused a good deal of awe and comment about the Annenberg style. The ambassador, for instance, was invited to a luncheon by a high-ranking British official who wanted to

give some cabinet officers the opportunity to meet him.
The affair was held in a private dining room and a dark-
haired Spanish waitress was about to begin serving when
Annenberg leaned toward his host and asked, "Would
you mind getting rid of the maid for a minute and closing
the door." The man immediately jumped up and asked
the waitress to leave, carefully bolting the door behind
her.

All eyes in the room suddenly turned toward Annenberg. There was obviously an important reason why he
wanted privacy. Everyone knew he was very close to
President Nixon and probably had access to important
information that might affect American-British relationships. Perhaps he was about to reveal some significant
change in American foreign policy or provide advance
knowledge of a forthcoming presidential pronouncement.

Annenberg looked slowly around the room, smiled a
bit, and asked: "Did you fellows ever head the one about
the girl who swam the Channel?"

Taken aback, his audience listened in mute bewilder-
ment while the American ambassador told in exquisite
detail a dirty joke.

○ ○ ○

In many ways, Annenberg didn't seem to change at all
in his prestigious new post. He was still prone to jump
to conclusions quickly and more than once displayed his
mercurial temperament. One minister kept him waiting
for ten minutes at their first meeting and Annenberg refused to forgive him for it, reportedly took to downgrad-

ing proposals which came in from that man's department, and told an aide, "I won't trust him again."

And, of course, his attitude toward the press hasn't changed much. Despite the fact that he himself was a major overlord in American journalism, he has always considered himself immune from the bothersome inquiries of the press and has often treated probing reporters with disdain. Following the national attention his ambassadorial appointment received, however, it appeared for a while that Annenberg was going to be forced to at last learn to live in the public spotlight.

That doesn't seem to be the case. The new American ambassador initially refused to hold press conferences or submit to in-depth interviews by the British press, American correspondents, or members of the foreign press corps in London. Reporters who early managed to corner him found themselves being tongue-lashed for what he considers the unfair treatment given him by the British newspapers. Annenberg's own attitude toward his press treatment is interesting if not uncharacteristic. A friend asked him what he thought the reason was for the kind of press reviews he was getting. "Well, you know how it is," he explained. "Any man in my position creates a good deal of envy."

Actually, the British papers were displaying an unusual amount of restraint. That may have been as a result of a letter from the British Foreign Office to England's press lords suggesting that their newspapers print no adverse quotes about Annenberg from British sources and that such comment from American sources be kept to a minimum. Nevertheless, an occasional editorial jibe could not be held back, as when the *Daily Mail* noted: "Walter Annenberg, the American Ambassador, can brighten up a bit. With his wife Leonore, he has been invited to Dorneywood for the weekend. This is the official country home of Michael Stewart, the Foreign Secretary. The invitation is one of the few nice things to have happened to Annenberg since he arrived in London. . . ."

What little comment there was in the press came, strangely enough, from what is normally considered the pro-American part of it. A particularly biting piece in the *Sunday Telegraph*, for instance, was headlined PROGRESS REPORT ON AMERICA'S AMBASSADOR and quoted a "keen observer of the diplomatic scene" as saying: "If you thought there had to be decisions about peace and war, Mr. Annenberg is not the kind of man you would choose to send to London." Concluded the report: "Unless Mr. Walter H. Annenberg makes a swift recovery and learns to cope with the difficult British, it is safe to forecast that most London-Washington business will soon be transacted in Washington."

Perhaps one of the reasons there wasn't more such criticism in the British press was that members of the Fleet Street brigade were finding it difficult to believe that their inability to reach the new American ambassador was due to Annenberg's own sensitivities. "He is, after all, a newspaperman himself, isn't he?" they were asking. Then when stories began circulating about the behavior of the new ambassador, they became more than ever certain there was a nefarious plot at the American embassy to keep him under wraps. "I should imagine," said one reporter, "that they've already told him, 'For heaven's sake, stay indoors!' "

*The Diplomatist,* ever diplomatic, put it this way: "What so many people wonder is why does a man with such strength of character permit himself to be controlled, checked, directed and played with by unknown diplomatic advisers to such an extent that within months he has become the object of a lot of amusement and not a little ill-will. . . . American officials and advisers seem to have taken hold of His Excellency upon his arrival in London with the same iron grip as that with which prison officials take hold of a newly arrived inmate who has a particularly bad record."

Walter Annenberg thought his appointment as ambassador to the Court of St. James's would finally give him that elusive sort of status and social acceptability his millions could not buy. He had bent his every effort, from the manner in which he controlled his communications empire to the direction of his philanthropy, to achieving that goal. Yet in his early months as ambassador, Annenberg was having a very difficult time establishing himself in the minds of many Englishmen as worthy of the respect usually afforded the post. There seemed to be developing, in fact, an attitude of irreverence toward him perhaps best exemplified by the gratuitous conclusion of that so-called "Progress Report" which appeared in the *Sunday Telegraph:* "Meanwhile," it noted, "there is talk of installing piped music in the Ambassadorial residence."

Annenberg, now remote from the powerful editorial

voices through which he might have once answered with vengeance thousands of miles away, must bear such barbs in public silence. He sits in his huge, austerely paneled office at the United States Embassy in London surrounded by the treasures and mementos of his successful career. A Gilbert Stuart portrait of George Washington and two Andrew Wyeth paintings which he brought from his home hang on the wall. Behind his desk are autographed photographs of Presidents Eisenhower, Johnson, and, of course, Nixon. There is also one from Winston Churchill. On a table nearby rests a large aerial color photo of his oasis haven in the desert of California, the warm, brightly sunlit landscape it depicts a contrast to the cool, gray dampness of the English atmosphere just outside the embassy's tall tinted windows. There are also a number of other plaques and awards, framed certificates and photographs scattered about, most of which Annenberg had brought with him from his old sanctuary, his twelfth-floor office in the *Inquirer* building. Finally, of course, there is the large mahogany-and-bronze plaque he had kept on a shelf close to his desk in Philadelphia, the one with the inscription he holds so dear: "Cause my works on earth to reflect honor on my father's memory."

Walter Annenberg would never forget that.

# (Last Add)

On October 28, 1969, a few minutes after three o'clock in the afternoon, Royal Plenty, the financial editor of the Philadelphia *Inquirer,* emerged from the daily meeting with managing editor John Gillen. It was a routine meeting at which each of the department editors discussed what the major stories in their sections would be the next day. No one mentioned anything especially exciting. On his way back to his office just off the city room, Plenty walked by the Dow Jones wire-service machine. He regularly checks it at least a couple of dozen times a day. Now it was chattering out the closing averages of the day's market prices. Plenty's eye, however, fell on two lines of caps that had come across just prior to the averages.

Royal Plenty is a big, rather taciturn man, balding, with thick glasses and a pleasantly round face. He has been in the newspaper business too long to get excited about anything. When he saw those two lines of purple type sitting on the broad tape of the ticker, he said in a soft, unemotional voice: "Hey, there's some pretty big news here."

Harry LaCroix, Plenty's assistant on the financial desk, saw him mumble something and called over: "What's that, Royal?"

"I said, 'Here's a pretty big story,'" said Plenty.

"What is it?"

"Come over and look at it."

"Just read it to me."

Royal Plenty read him the headline: KNIGHT PAPERS PURCHASES PHILADELPHIA INQUIRER AND PHILADELPHIA DAILY NEWS.

In a few minutes the city room of the *Inquirer* was in a state of semi-chaos. The operations desk, normally a smoothly functioning control center for assignments and copy, completely broke down. Staffers began wandering around excitedly repeating the news to each other. In a place that had always been, in the words of one reporter, "a very sophisticated rumor mill," not a hint of the sale had been heard. Even city editor Harry Belinger looked shocked. And unbelieving surprise was the expression on the faces of most of the *Inquirer* staffers as they gathered around the bulletin board where Newspaper Guild vice president Jim Young had posted the wire copy.

Down through the years there had been rumors here and there in Philadelphia's gossip circles that Annenberg's newspapers were hurting financially and that he was thinking of selling them. But there are rumors about everything and no knowledgeable person ever took them seriously. The gossiping, however, reached a peak about the time of the announcement of his appointment as ambassador and on February 21, 1969, this box appeared on page three of the *Inquirer*:

Walter H. Annenberg, editor and publisher of The Philadelphia Inquirer, has issued the following statement:

"There are rumors to the effect that The Philadelphia Inquirer is being sold.

"These rumors are utterly without foundation in fact.

"I have no intention whatever of disposing of The Philadelphia Inquirer, or the Philadelphia Daily News."

Seven months later the staffs of his two newspapers were staring in amazement at a piece of wire-service copy tacked on a bulletin board which said that Walter Annenberg had sold out.

The *Inquirer* of October 29, 1969, carried the news as the number one story on its front page. The sale, it said, had been announced the day before "in a joint statement by Ambassador Walter H. Annenberg of Triangle Publications and John S. Knight, editorial chairman and senior officer of Knight Newspapers.

"The consideration was approximately $55,000,000 in cash and notes."

The transfer of ownership was scheduled for final closing on December 31, 1969. The two Philadelphia papers would make the Knight group of newspapers the third largest in the country, behind Newhouse and Scripps-Howard, in total weekly circulation.

Lee Hills, president and executive editor of Knight Newspapers, said that Annenberg will have the title of "Editor and Publisher Emeritus" of the *Inquirer* and that "he has agreed to be available for consultation after completing his government service."

Hills, however, stressed the long-standing Knight policy and practice of local autonomy. "Individual editors are responsible for the news and editorial policies of their newspapers to insure that they serve the best interests of their communities," he said. "We do not operate by directives from any headquarters."

When the shock from the announcement of the sale

had worn off, speculation about *why* Annenberg had sold his newspapers began. In a statement that appeared on the front page of the *Inquirer,* Annenberg himself said:

"My decision to sell The Philadelphia Inquirer and The Daily News was made to accomplish an orderly transfer into the right hands of the newspapers that have long been under my direction.

"With the passing of my only son, there is no likely possibility of family transference, and hence my desire to insure a future ownership in which I have confidence."

There were other factors, however, not in the statement, which may have influenced Annenberg's decision. He had, for instance, privately confided shortly after his appointment as ambassador that he was thinking of eventually making Triangle Publications a public concern. Without an heir to hand the reins to, he said, that was his only course. The sale of the *Inquirer* and *Daily News,* the least profitable of any of its operations, would make Triangle one of the financially strongest corporations in the country and a very attractive stock tender.

Yet it is difficult to believe that financial considerations alone would have led Annenberg to dispose of the *Inquirer*. His other holdings were strictly business ventures. He had gotten into *TV Guide* and *Seventeen* and his radio and television stations primarily for the thrill and excitement of making a shrewd dollar. But the *Inquirer* was rarely, if ever, a big money-maker. That mattered little to Walter Annenberg over the years. What mattered most was that it was his father's legacy. That, and his own power and prestige. It was the instrument with which he could right the dishonor wrought upon his father's name.

Didn't he do exactly that? Didn't he achieve in his appointment as ambassador to the Court of St. James's *the* consummate social and public distinction for the Annenberg name?

And yet for the first time in his life he was being subjected to the kind of public examination and criticism he had never experienced before. And a good deal of it had to do with his record as editor and publisher of the *Inquirer*. Milton Shapp, for instance, the Pennsylvania gubernatorial candidate on whom Annenberg had ordered the vicious editorial hatchet job in the 1966 election, filed with the Federal Communications Commission in July, 1969, an objection to the renewal of the license of Annenberg's profitable Philadelphia television station. "Renewal of the Triangle license is not in the public interest," said Shapp, "because this company exercises a near news monopoly in the Philadelphia area, and because over the years the record shows that the company's handling of the news is distinctly not in the public interest."

Perhaps Annenberg could have called upon presidential influence, but the FCC had not long ago broken precedent by taking away the license of a Boston television station from the Boston *Herald-Traveler* on the grounds of monopoly. It would have been a great humiliation to Annenberg to lose the valuable WFIL license at the petition of Milton Shapp, a man he had once blatantly and brutally interred.

And part of Shapp's documentation to back his claim of Triangle's lack of primary concern for the public interest was Annenberg's record of handling the *Inquirer*.

That record also figured strongly at Annenberg's hearings before the Senate Foreign Relations Committee in Washington.

Too, it was beginning to be examined more closely by the British press and hindering Annenberg's efforts to achieve the diplomatic regard afforded his predecessor.

In sum, the Philadelphia *Inquirer* was no longer a personally rewarding or prestigious asset for Walter Annenberg.

∘ ∘ ∘

It is not insignificant that the dominant mood in the city rooms of the *Inquirer* and *Daily News,* once the initial impact of the announcement of their sale had subsided, eventually turned to jubilation. "It is like being traded in August from a last place team to a pennant contender," one reporter said happily. City editor Belinger had a tough time bringing the *Inquirer* city room staffers down from their cloud, and finally began shouting to individual deskmen to get back to work.

Downstairs on the seventh floor of the Inquirer Building where the *Daily News* lives, word of the sale broke less spectacularly. Joe O'Dowd, a police reporter, had intercepted a call for his *Inquirer* colleague at the Police Administration Building. Quickly he called the news back to his own city room. Tom Cooney, the *News*'s city editor, laughed at him. He wasn't going to believe anything that crazy, he said, and dismissed O'Dowd's report.

At about the same time a call came in for reporter Tom

Fox from a man who said he was a friend of his on the Akron, Ohio, *Beacon Journal*. Fox was not at work and the desk would not give the caller Fox's home number. The man demanded the number. No dice. Finally he said: "I absolutely demand Fox's number. I want to discuss with him the sale of the *Inquirer* and *Daily News* to the Knight organization!"

That got action. The desk called Fox at home and told him a reporter friend of his in Akron had been trying to reach him. Fox called his friend and learned about the sale just as confirmation of it was reaching the *Daily News*. A copy boy whose name, incidentally, is Steve Wilson, saw news of the sale being typed out on the United Press International machine. At first, the significance of the words didn't click and he didn't say anything about it. Finally he mentioned it to someone on the desk who jumped up, ran to the machine and began to shout: "Oh my God! This is unbelievable! Unbelievable! He *sold* it! He *sold* it!"

A lot of noise and shouting quickly broke out. Some, however, were just too stunned to react. Sports columnist Stan Hochman sat silently at his typewriter and slowly a small smile crossed his face. J. Ray Hunt, the legendary red-faced Irishman who long managed the *Daily News,* had been called to a meeting upstairs and no one caught his immediate reaction. When he returned, however, he was equal to the moment.

"Everyone gather round, gather round," he snapped in his best patriarchal tone. The staff obeyed. Hunt, wisps of white hair astray, a touch of gleam in his eye, cigar in mouth, newspapers under his arm, began. He was taking inspiration from the great Knute Rockne, who had coached at Notre Dame when Hunt attended.

"You all know the newspaper has been sold," said Hunt. "Now this is just one little guy's opinion, just one guy, but I think it's a good move. The Knights put out quality papers. I knew John Knight in Detroit and I knew him in Chicago. I know his brother Jim. I don't want anybody to fret or worry because I think this means growth. I think it means growth for us all. It will be better than working for an absentee publisher. I think they're going to take the damn handcuffs off us."

He went on like that, making one of the great speeches of his career while slightly out of earshot one of his reporters remarked, "Christ, I wish I had a tape recorder. This would be great to get on tape."

Then Hunt closed with a line that may become a classic in the paper's city room lore: "Of course," he said, "all of this doesn't take effect until the first of January. So what I want to say now is . . . *Happy New Year!*"

There were a number of others on both papers who wanted to shout but didn't. From that distance, the New Year didn't seem that close, and who can tell what can happen in these terribly complex big business deals? Some, however, did express their reaction in various subtle ways.

There was, for instance, a clock in the office of *Inquirer* managing editor John Gillen. When Walter Annenberg assumed his post as ambassador to Great Britain, someone, possibly in jest, put the clock on London time. The day after the papers were sold it was back on Philadelphia time.

# Index